W9-AOY-776

HISTORY AND HOPE

CONTRIBUTORS

Kathleen Bliss, A.K. Brohi
Pieter Geyl, Jeanne Hersch
Sidney Hook, Albert Hourani
Theodor Litt, Richard Lowenthal
Herbert Lüthy, Salvador de Madariaga
Ehsan Naraghi, Jayaprakash Narayan
Robert Oppenheimer, Joseph Pieper
Michael Polanyi, Raja Rao
Ronald Segal, Michio Takeyama
and others

HISTORY
AND HOPE

TRADITION, IDEOLOGY, AND CHANGE

IN MODERN SOCIETY

Edited by
K. A. Jelenski

—

With a Postscript by
Michael Polanyi

Essay Index Reprint Series

 BOOKS FOR LIBRARIES PRESS
FREEPORT, NEW YORK

Reprinted 1970 by arrangement with Praeger Publishers, Inc.

INTERNATIONAL STANDARD BOOK NUMBER:

0-8369-1794-4

LIBRARY OF CONGRESS CATALOG CARD NUMBER:

70-117773

PRINTED IN THE UNITED STATES OF AMERICA

CONTENTS

v

Contents

Introduction

K. A. JELENSKI

THE last decade witnessed a growing awareness in Europe of the exhaustion of the nineteenth-century ideologies. Two chains of events lie behind this important change. One is formed by the catastrophes and delusions of the earlier two decades, the years between 1930 and 1950, which brought about a decline of millenarian doctrines. The other is connected with the rise of the Welfare State, with the modifications of capitalism, the matter-of-fact fulfilment of some of the aims of socialism, and with a growing realization that the realities of industrialism are perhaps a more important determining factor socially than political systems, whatever their ideological origin.

The Berlin Conference of 1960, held on the tenth anniversary of the foundation of the Congress for Cultural Freedom, brought together more than two hundred scholars, writers and intellectuals in discussions on the principal problems of this decade, under the central theme of 'Tradition and Change'. While other study groups at the Berlin conference were concerned with the political, sociological and cultural aspects of this theme, the seminar directed by Professor Michael Polanyi was devoted to the 'Progress of Ideas'. *History and Hope* contains the papers presented at this seminar and excerpts from the discussion which followed.

Professor Polanyi's introductory paper, 'Beyond Nihilism', contains a challenging and hopeful view of the ideological evolution of our time. Polanyi considers the revisionist movement which manifested itself in Poland and in Hungary from 1954 onwards, and which culminated in the Polish October of 1956 and in the Hungarian revolution as an historical landmark equal in importance to the French Revolution. Indeed, in Polanyi's interpretation, 'revisionism' is not merely the neo-Marxist reaction to Stalinist totalitarianism set in motion by

1

young Polish and Hungarian Communists, but, in a much wider sense, a reflection in the West as well as in the Communist world—of the receding influence of the chiliastic ideologies on intellectuals, and on public opinion in general.

'Beyond Nihilism' is a study of the rising tide of this 'moral inversion' which Polanyi associates with modern ideologies; of its recession; and of the new landmarks (which are perhaps but new forms of old ones), which this recession uncovers. Among these landmarks, Polanyi recognizes 'a reawakened national feeling', 'a new alliance between liberalism and religious beliefs', and a new lease of life given to the sceptical mood of the enlightenment itself.

There is a genuine possibility by which men may discover an avenue which will not lead back into nihilism:

'Perhaps the present recoil may be stabilized by the upsurge of a more clear-sighted political conscience. We might conceivably achieve a kind of suspended logic, like that which kept England and America so happily backward on the road to disaster. . . . Civility prevailed in England over religious strife and a society was founded which was dynamic and yet united. May not Europe repeat this feat? May we not learn from the disaster of the last forty years to establish a civic partnership, united in its resolve on continuous reforms—our dynamism restrained by the knowledge that radicalism will throw us back into disaster the moment we try to act out its principles literally?'

Polanyi's essay served to guide much of the subsequent course of the discussion. His thesis that both Communism and Nazism are two forms of modern nihilistic fanaticism which he sees as a perverted consequence of the Enlightenment, was criticized by Richard Lowenthal who insisted on essential differences between Marx and his followers on the one hand, and Fascists and National Socialists on the other, and by Sidney Hook who refused to see in the Enlightenment anything else than the origin of modern rationalism.

Three major themes raised in the ensuing discussion were:

1. The ideological, social and historical origins of the two great 'secular fanaticisms' of our time: Communism and Fascism; their similarities and differences.

2. The declaration of the end of ideology, and, as evidence: the revisionism in Europe, the exhaustion of ideological interest

2

in the Western world, the erosion or routinization of ideological fervour in post-Stalinist Soviet Russia.

3. The prospects for a post-authoritarian, non-ideological society of the future, for what Polanyi calls 'a new civility': Does this envisage a return to a progressive, reformist liberal society, with a pragmatic attitude toward public affairs? Or does it imply a reaffirmation of pre-Enlightenment values, characteristic of traditional societies: national feeling, religious belief?

I. The Secular Fanaticisms of our Time

Before the Age of Enlightenment, societies did not nourish the secular design of transforming society fundamentally or of achieving social perfection, while after the Age of Enlightenment societies tended to become dynamic, obsessed with the concept of progress and change, and intent on achieving the goals of perfection 'here and now'.

What are the intellectual conditions under which both communism and fascism have gained power over the minds of men? Michael Polanyi has emphasized secularization itself—Man's attempt to conceive the meaning of life in this world in immanent terms. Richard Lowenthal stressed a different condition: the emergence of the democratic concept in the broadest sense of the word, the idea that the political and social order could be no longer regarded as God-given and must derive its sanction from the will of the people. 'All totalitarian ideologies [says Lowenthal] are based on the fiction that the totalitarian movement represents the true will of the people, the *volonté générale* in Rousseau's sense.' And he adds: 'The very idea of a totalitarian political movement gaining power and then continuing to mobilize the masses for the purposes of its régime is only conceivable in an age where a democratic legitimation has become indispensable for every régime.'

Lowenthal mentions two other major intellectual conditions for the rise of the revolutionary historical myths: the conscious experience of historic change and the confidence, engendered by the progress of science, in the scientific predictability of the natural order, which is then extended to the field of history.

Thus, secularization, the democratic principle of legitimacy, the experience of historic change and the belief in its scientific predictability, which are all implicit in the intellectual revolution

3

of the Age of Enlightenment, form the indispensable background to the totalitarian ideologies of our time. But they also form the general intellectual background, since the end of the eighteenth century, to the new 'dynamic' societies of today.

At another seminar organized by the Congress for Cultural Freedom at Rheinfelden, near Basle, in 1959, Michael Polanyi made a distinction between two kinds of contemporary dynamic society: the reformist, progressive society, and the totalitarian society:

'What opposes these two types of dynamic societies, is their attitude towards human nature, the nature of truth, their ideas about human goodness, honesty, etc. Progressive society has no reason to distrust these ideas, since it lets itself be guided, little by little, by their manifestations which it considers as authentic factors for the amelioration of society. Totalitarian society is much more influenced by the union of science as a guide to reality with Messianic aims and I think its relation towards ideas is fundamentally inverted ...'

This statement contains an implication of the thesis Polanyi develops in 'Beyond Nihilism':

'I believe [he says] that never in the history of mankind has the hunger for brotherhood and righteousness exercised such power over the minds of men as today. The past two centuries have not been an age of moral weakness, but have, on the contrary, seen outbreaks of a moral fervour which has achieved numberless humanitarian reforms and has improved modern society beyond the boldest thought of earlier centuries. And I believe that it is this fervour which in our own lifetime has outreached itself by its inordinate aspirations and thus heaped on mankind the disasters that have befallen us ... We have yet to discover the proper terms for describing this event. Ethics must catch up with the pathological forms of morals due to the modern intensification of morality. We must learn to recognize moral excesses.'

But, even if elements of 'moral inversion' were implicitly present in the secular urge towards perfection which first manifested itself in the Age of Enlightenment, the fact still remains that the same intellectual background gave birth to two different kinds of modern societies—the reformist and the totalitarian. Participants of the study-group sought specific causes of the rise of totalitarianism: religious, sociological, historical.

4

One of the implications of secularization, the transfer of the religious urge to problems of this world, was particularly stressed. J. L. Talmon, author of *The Origins of Totalitarian Democracy*, thus underlined the 'para-religious' character of political Messianism at the seminar of Rheinfelden: 'The principal characteristic of Messianic thinkers and theoreticians, from Rousseau to Marx, passing through Saint-Simon, Fourier and others, is that each one of them finds it absolutely necessary to begin his research and to continue it through a *réglement de comptes* with religion. They are all entirely, I would say aggressively, conscious of offering a substitute to religion.'

Following this line of argument, Richard Lowenthal attaches particular importance to the secularization of the religious hope of the Millennium: 'There is more than "moral passion" in an elaborate system that tells us that mankind started in a state of innocence (state of nature, primitive Communism), was corrupted by ambition and avarice (class society, state, exploitation) and will eventually enter a realm of perfect justice where all sin (oppression, exploitation, rivalry) and conflict will disappear and no compulsion will be needed: this is a sacred history and a promise of salvation on earth.' We are here faced with a modern version of the chiliastic heresies of the Middle Ages. Lowenthal goes on to show that Nazi doctrine is just such a perverted reflection of millenarianism: 'The formal structure of their vision of history showed the same origin in the tripartite apocalyptic scheme as that of their Marxist antipodes, with biology replacing economics as the master-key to history, the state of innocence identified with racial purity and the fall with the bastardization of the fallen race.' But its spiritual model is to be found not in chiliastic, but in antinomian and satanistic heresies: 'those which sought to escape from the burden of guilt and moral conflict in the doctrine that every "sin" was permitted to the Elect, and that the ability to commit deeds which to others were deadly sin without a sense of guilt was the very proof of election'.

Richard Lowenthal also developed in his paper what he called the 'dynamic' causes for the rise of totalitarianism, which can be described as the collapse of traditional authority in a society where rules of conduct are dependent on external authority both for their preservation and their gradual adjustment to changing conditions.

Sidney Hook, however, rejected the entire set of presuppositions in the arguments of Polanyi and Lowenthal: 'The chief causes of the Bolshevik and Nazi revolutions have very little to do with doctrinal beliefs. They are to be found in the First World War and its consequences. Not 1789 but 1914 deserves the title of the Year of the Second Fall of Man.'

A considerable part of the discussion was concerned with doing away with a misunderstanding which arose out of Polanyi's interpretation of Communism and Nazism as two forms of moral nihilistic inversion. Certainly the totalitarianism of the left and the totalitarianism of the right are two different kinds of revolt against the hypocrisy of the old order. And certainly the manifestations of both were similarly callous and cruel. But while Marx and his followers attacked 'bourgeois morality' as hypocritical, they attacked it from the basis of its own professed universal values: of the Judaeo-Christian and liberal-humanist tradition. In fact, the revisionist 'revolution' was a reaction against a new hypocrisy, undertaken in the defence of values which the Communists still professed in doctrine while disregarding them in practice. Fascists and National Socialists, on the other hand, start from a similar disgust with the old order, but they conclude that these values themselves are false and should be replaced by an 'honest' cult of the stronger, the ennobling qualities of violence and the rejection of all traditional moral restraints in principle.

Whatever the differences of theory, however, Theodor Litt's testimony of his own experiences under Nazism and under Communism in Eastern Germany demonstrated the existence in both of the same mixture of the rational and the irrational, of 'exasperated moral passion' and nihilism which Polanyi diagnosed in his paper.

II. The End of the Ideological Age?

However much disagreement there was as to their causes, there was considerable agreement that evidence of the end of ideologies does exist.

Let us first examine Polish and Hungarian revisionism and Polanyi's implication that revisionism is tied to a revival of national and religious feeling.

If by 'revisionism' we understand the voice of the *pays réel* which first expressed itself after years of repression and silence, then Polanyi's contention is right: events in Poland and in Hungary showed that nationalism and religion are still strong. But if we consider 'revisionism' in its strict terms, if we apply it only to the Polish and Hungarian *Communist* writers, philosophers, intellectuals who revolted against the discrepancy between the professed humanistic values and the inhuman totalitarian practice of the régime, then the return to patriotic and religious values is far less evident. Polish revisionists rediscovered the crucial fact which degraded Marxism into the Communist totalitarian ideology—this was Lenin's 1902 dogma of 'democratic centralism', of the identification of 'the Proletariat' with 'the Party' which must at all costs preserve total power. These revisionists were returning to the ideas of Rosa Luxemburg, under whose influence the Polish Communist Party had been originally formed, of 'Workers' Democracy' and of internationalism. These ideas were overtly stressed in numerous essays which appeared in *Po Prostu*, the magazine of the youthful Polish revisionists. While they could never say so directly, Polish revisionists often implied that Poland's independence from the Soviet Union was to be defended not merely on 'patriotic' grounds, but in order to form a sort of 'bridgehead' of new internationalism.

The attitude of Polish revisionists towards religion had an ambiguous character, and does not entirely justify Polanyi's claim that 'another revisionist idea lay in the newly-found alliance between liberalism and religious beliefs'. Polish revisionists were virulent anticlericals. But they rightly perceived that religious persecution had greatly strengthened the position of the Catholic Church in Poland. They called for religious tolerance not out of any sympathy for religion, but because (*a*) they considered Stalinism the worst form of clericalism and (*b*) they did in fact return to many ideas of the Age of Enlightenment, and briefly regained faith in the force of reason. But Polish revisionists became gradually aware of their inefficacy. Their attempt to re-think Communism in genuinely Marxist terms, their desire to see how one could bring about a true Communist society in contrast to the monstrosities of Stalinism, were short-lived. Most revisionists became disillusioned and sceptical. The majority has probably arrived at what one might call approximately 'social democratic' conclusions. Most of them share the hope, widespread in the West, that the transformation of the Soviet Union into an industrial society will make it possible to arrive at some equivalent of a democratic welfare state. A small minority has come to consider that traditional values such as the nation or religious beliefs are the only effective bulwarks against modern totalitarianism. It may be that Polanyi's conclusions apply to this minority only and that this minority turned to pragmatic traditionalism after 1957, that is as a consequence of the apparent failure of their revisionist movement. But this may be a problem of vocabulary: one can, as in the foregoing, interpret 'revisionism' in the narrow sense of the neo-Marxist thought which manifested itself in the Communist bloc between 1954 and 1957, and which since has been silenced.

One thing is certain: The Polish and Hungarian revisionists refused to sacrifice the present of mankind for a promised tomorrow; as a result of their experience with that 'future', they did assert the claims of humanism.

As the foremost Polish revisionist philosopher Leszek Kolakowski put it:

'I shall never believe that the moral and intellectual life of mankind conforms to the laws of economic investments, that is, that one should expect better results tomorrow by saving today, i.e. use lies for the triumph of truth and take advantage of crime in order to pave the way for righteousness.'

The evidence pointing to the end of ideologies in the West has been reduced by most speakers to the visible exhaustion of ideological interest in the post-war Western world, and particularly among the young generations. But since we are here concerned with ideas and with the intellectuals who have been the bearers of ideologies, the existence of small revisionist groups in the West may be relevant. Like *Po Prostu* or the *Irodalmi Ujsag* of 1956 in Poland and Hungary, the English *New Left Review*, the French *Arguments*, the American *Dissent* have obviously abandoned the doctrinaire interpretation of orthodox Marxism and have in common a search for a new socialist humanism. Surely it is significant that the most radical young intellectuals in the West seem to have lost a Messianic faith in the proletariat and do not even strike out with any self-assurance against 'the capitalists' or 'the bourgeoisie'. The new target of their criticism is rather the amorphous 'mass society', which they attack in the language of early Marx, particularly in terms of alienation.

Indeed, what may account for the changed temper of even the most dissatisfied elements of Western contemporary intelligentsia, is that their discontent is expressed within the framework of a highly organized industrial society, in which the terms of the class struggle, as laid down by Marx, have lost much of their relevance. Western revisionists may refuse to see that the socio-economic mutation of the societies in which they live can be interpreted in marxist terms as realising some of Marx's own hopes, although not along the lines of his prophecies; that class division can one day be abolished not through the victory of the proletariat over the bourgeoisie, but by both of them merging in a 'mass society'. But even if some of them continue to reject this interpretation of contemporary changes, they no longer believe in a proletarian revolution which will bring about the Millennium. The most stubborn Manicheans among them now tend to identify themselves with the former colonial peoples, who, in their view have inherited revolutionary dynamics previously attributed to the proletariat.

What seems certain, however, is that the image of the Millennium has generally lost its sway and so has the feeling that all means are acceptable if in the long run they will bring it about. If there is no certitude about what is the ultimate image of the new society, pragmatic compromise begins anew to be considered as the least of all evils.

What Karl Popper calls 'piecemeal social engineering', the matter-of-fact, immediate problems of standard of living, education, etc., does, in fact, function in the West. As Michael Polanyi has pointed out in his paper, 'the more sober, pragmatist attitude towards public affairs which has spread since 1950 through England and America, Germany and Austria, reproduces in its repudiation of ideological strife the attitude of Voltaire and the Encyclopaedists towards religious bigotry'. But this perspective on society and politics is not exciting for intellectuals.

The young generation in the West has often been described as sober, matter-of-fact, having a 'mature' acceptance of politics and existence; but also as having an underlying restlessness, a feeling of being cheated out of an adventure, and a search for passion. They would probably agree with Max Weber that 'he

9

who seeks the salvation of souls, his own as well as others, should not seek it along the avenue of politics'. But where then, if at all, if he must, does contemporary man seek his 'salvation'? The irrational implications of this question may be decisive for the prospects of the post-authoritarian, post-ideological society evoked in Professor Polanyi's paper.

Can we speak of 'the end of ideology' in relation to the newly-emancipated 'underdeveloped countries', on whose evolution, in the long run, the future of our world may depend? Michael Polanyi said that the new intellectual movement which he connects with the Hungarian Revolution has, in less dramatic forms, 'spread all through the area of receding dynamism, almost everywhere outside Communist China'. He thinks that the 're-awakened national feeling rejuvenated the ancient societies of Asia and Africa, creating, along with much wasteful strife, new popular communities which transcend the ideological conflicts of European dynamism'.

The exception was stressed by Richard Lowenthal when he said 'Chinese Communism achieved total domination of a potential Great Power in 1949 after more than twenty years of civil war—at a time when, in Polanyi's view, the ideological age was already on its way out—and has shown an unexampled ideological virulence in recent years.'

As for the other rising States of Asia and Africa, it can be argued that they are fashioning new ideologies with a specific appeal for their own people, industrialization, modernization, race, Pan-Arabism and nationalism—which have a distant relationship to the old nineteenth-century ideologies which have become exhausted in the West. This relationship, according to J. L. Talmon (Seminar of Rheinfelden), rests on the fact that in Asia and Africa we are confronted with a new form of political Messianism. The nineteenth-century European version of political Messianism combined two postulates, according to Talmon: the desire to combat all alienation, and on the other hand the desire for cohesion, for organization. The differences of religious, spiritual, intellectual and political traditions in the West and in the new States of Asia and Africa lead Talmon to question the results of this 'transplantation' of a new form of political Messianism to other civilizations: 'Will they not be reduced to adopt its organizational aspect only, a sort of instrument to construct immense power-machines, while abandoning its prophetic disquiet, its prophetic mission? In this case, if we bear in mind that in the long run nationalistic particularities have proved more powerful, infinitely stronger than Messianic universalism, could we not fear that in adopting this sort of organizational Messianism, these civilizations, if they really neglect the prophetic tradition, may transform Messianism into a mere lever to construct instruments of power to extol their unique character, their differences, and to reject Western civilization, guilty of so much oppression in the past?'

III. Prospects for a Post-Ideological Society

Whatever particular objections and doubts were raised by some participants of the study-group, the moral and intellectual temper of the fifties at least in Europe and North America clearly indicates the abatement of nineteenth-century ideologies. The importance of Polanyi's challenge consists in the fact that he wishes to look beyond and study the next stage of the historical process in which we are involved.

At the Rheinfelden Seminar Polanyi mentioned another possible direction in which a post-authoritarian, post-ideological society might move: 'There is absolutely no reason for rejecting the eventualities of the replacement of modern fanatical societies, and of the corruption they bring about, by a reformist society.'

'Revisionism' might thus entail a return to a pre-Enlightenment view of the world (religion, nationalism), in fact to some degree to what Polanyi called an 'ancient and static society' But it might also entail a return to a conception of a reformist, progressive, liberal society which we owe to the Enlightenment.

Both these prospects were discussed by the study-group. Herbert Lüthy pointed out the ambiguity of nationalism in Polanyi's paper 'once as a fanatic ideology, another time as a form of hope'. He went on to warn against the latter approach: 'In recent years'—he says—'Titoism, the East German rising of 1953, the Hungarian and Polish revolutions of 1956, the Tibetan rising and similar events have led to a kind of rehabilitation of nationalism in Western thought. This is, in the first instance, merely an expression of relief at the fact that the Soviet system is also having trouble with nationalistic reactions, and of the understandable sympathy with every form of reaction to an equally brutal and deceitful despotism. Yet I nevertheless consider it important that we should not develop a double-mindedness with regard to a pathological phenomenon which, when it appears in the West, we regard as a plague, but of which, when it breaks out in the Communist Empire, we approve simply because it causes disquiet to the Communist rulers behind the Iron Curtain.'

Are we then to count nationalism among those manifestations of revisionism which could lead us beyond ideological religions towards a peaceful, tolerant and equilibrated society? Lüthy thinks our answer to this question should take into account two series of events: the fight for independence of the ex-colonial peoples and the awakening of nationalism in the Communist sphere of influence.

All the participants of the seminar expressed their unequivocal approval of the new independence movements in Asia and Africa. However, to what extent is our knowledge of European nationalism of any use in the effort to estimate the exact significance of other, non-European nationalisms? An answer to this question is important if we are to take the just measure of the vast revolution going on in the greater part of the world today.

As for the nationalist revival in the Eastern European revolutions, it was not their aim to establish a specifically Polish or Hungarian social order: it was a search for a new form of a just and free society. 'That this fight should have taken a nationalistic colour' [says Lüthy] 'is understandable, because every historic fight is taking place not in a no-man's-land of abstract humanity, but in the given framework of state institutions, of institutional possibilities inherent in political strife.' The demand for autonomy by cultural, religious, or even simply regional communities, for individual freedom of thought and behaviour permitting individuals as well as historical and social groups to breathe and develop freely, is not in essence nationalistic. In Lüthy's words: 'If we repudiate nationalism as a doctrine, as a principle of integration, this does not mean that any particular community has no right to live, but, on the contrary, that this right should be fully acknowledged.' Lüthy's solution to this problem, which was shared by Jeanne Hersch and other participants, is a federal and supra-national one: 'Today the Western world is beginning slowly and unwillingly to feel its way towards both pluralistic and supra-national forms of organization. There is as yet no indication of a definite success in this direction. Yet it is my firm conviction that no other method has any future, and that retreat would be catastrophic.'

It is characteristic that none of the contributors to this seminar seem to recognize the relevance of ideological and political categories of the last century, such as Left and Right, liberal and socialist, revolutionary and traditionalist. The conflicts which these categories imply have either become reconciled by experience or else so entangled that they can be detected in every camp. Didn't Stalin deplore in 1952 his followers' belief that the 'objective laws of economics'—that is the laws of the market—could be rendered invalid under socialism? Didn't the general acceptance in the West of the Keynesian model render the liberal theory of economic self-adjustment invalid? Can one describe as 'extreme left' the Soviet régime which identifies society with the State? What is the right ideological or political term for the new régimes of Asia and Africa which have had such an important bearing on the discussion?

To the new problems which are facing us today on a universal scale, a new approach is needed. The Berlin Conference was an attempt by philosophers, writers and scholars of four continents, united by a common bond of attachment to freedom, to find a new approach.

PART I

Beyond the Ideological Passions?

Beyond Nihilism

MICHAEL POLANYI

WE are told that moral improvement has not kept pace with the advance of science, and that the troubles of our age are largely due to this disparity. I shall argue that this view is false, or at least profoundly misleading. For I believe that never in the history of mankind has the hunger for brotherhood and righteousness exercised such power over the minds of men as today. The past two centuries have not been an age of moral weakness, but have, on the contrary, seen the outbreak of a moral fervour which has achieved numberless humanitarian reforms and has improved modern society beyond the boldest thoughts of earlier centuries. And I believe that it is this fervour which in our own lifetime has outreached itself by its inordinate aspirations and thus heaped on mankind the disasters that have befallen us. I admit that these disasters were accompanied by moral depravation. But I deny that this justifies us in speaking of moral retardation. What sluggish river has ever broken the dams which contained it or smashed the wheels which harnessed it? We have yet to discover the proper terms for describing this event. Ethics must catch up with the pathological forms of morals due to the modern intensification of morality. We must learn to recognize moral excesses.

I shall suggest that modern nihilism is a moral excess from which we are suffering today. And I shall try to look past this stage and see whether there is in fact anything beyond it. For our passion for nihilistic self-doubt may be incurable, and it may come to an end only when it has finally destroyed our civilization.

To speak of moral passions is something new. The idea that morality consists in imposing on ourselves the curb of moral commands, is so ingrained in us, that we simply cannot see that

17

the moral need of our time is, on the contrary, to curb our inordinate moral demands, which precipitate us into moral degradation and threaten us with bodily destruction.

There is admittedly one ancient record of moral admonitions which are outbreaks of moral passions: the sermons of the Hebrew prophets. I might have disregarded these since their fulminations were fired by religious zeal and the religious zeal of Judaeo-Christianity is not primarily moral. But these prophetic utterances are relevant here because their Messianism, reinforced by the apocalyptic messages of the New Testament, gave rise in the late Middle Ages and after, to a series of chiliastic outbursts in which the inversion of moral passions into nihilism made its first appearance.

This has been followed up recently by Norman Cohn in *The Pursuit of the Millennium*. He shows that the initial impetus to the repeated Messianic rebellions, which occurred in Central Europe from the eleventh to the sixteenth centuries was given by the great moral reforms of Gregory VII. His violent resolve to purge the Church of simony, to prohibit the marriage of the clergy and enforce their chastity retrieved the Church from imminent decay, but it did so at the cost of inciting the populace to rebellion against the clergy. These rebellions were both religious and moral. Their master ideas could be conceived only in a Christian society, for they assailed the spiritual rulers of society for offending against their own teachings. Rulers who did not preach Christian ideals could not be attacked in these terms.[1]

Since no society can live up to Christian precepts, any society professing Christian precepts must be afflicted by an internal contradiction, and when the tension is released by rebellion its agents must tend to establish a nihilist Messianic rule. For a victorious rising will create a new centre of power, and as the rising had been motivated by Christian morality, the new centre will be beset by the same contradiction against which its supporters had risen in rebellion. It will, indeed, be in a worse position, for its internal balance will not be protected by any customary compromise. It can then hold on only by proclaiming

[1] I am concerned here only with risings proclaiming moral principles which the existing rulers profess, and are accused of failing to observe. This does not apply generally to outbursts of millenarism among primitive people. Even so, such movements are most frequently induced by the teachings of Christian missionaries. (See Peter Worsley, *The Trumpet Sounds*, London 1957, p. 245.)

18

itself to be the absolute good : a Second Coming greater than the first and placed therefore beyond good and evil. We see arising then the 'moral superman', whom Norman Cohn compares with the 'armed bohemians' of our days, the followers of Bakunin and Nietzsche. For the first time the excesses of Christian morality turned here into fierce immoralism.

But these events were but scattered prodromal signs. The full power of the disturbance which had caused them became manifest only after the secularization of Europe in the eighteenth century. This change was neither sudden nor complete: but secularization was broadly completed in half a century. It was decisively advanced by the new scientific outlook; the victory of Voltaire over Bossuet was the triumph of Newton, even though Newton might not have wanted it. The scientific revolution supplied the supreme axiom of eighteenth-century rationalism, the rejection of all authority; *Nullius in Verba* had been the motto of the Royal Society at its foundation in 1660. Science served also as a major example for emancipating knowledge from religious dogma.

The new world view was expected to set man free to follow the natural light of reason, and thus to put an end to religious fanaticism and bigotry which were deemed the worst misfortunes of mankind. Humanity would advance then peacefully towards ever higher intellectual, moral, political and economic perfection. But already quite early in the development of this perspective—almost forty years before universal progress was first envisaged by Condorcet—Rousseau had challenged its hopes in his *Discourse on the Arts and Sciences* (1750) and *Discourse on Inequality* (1754). He declared that civilized man was morally degenerate, for he lives only outside himself, by the good opinion of others. He was a 'hollow man', an 'other directed person', to use terms coined two centuries later. Rousseau actually attributed this degeneration 'to the progress of the human mind', which had produced inequalities and consolidated them by the establishment of property. Man's original virtue had thus been corrupted and his person enslaved. Here is moral fury attacking all that is of good repute: all accepted manners, custom and law; exalting instead a golden age which was before good and evil.

Admittedly, his fervent dedication of the *Discourse on Inequality* to the city of Geneva shows that Rousseau's text was vastly hyperbolic. Yet by his argument and rhetoric he poured into the channels of rationalism a fierce passion for humanity. His thought so widened these channels that they could be fraught eventually with all the supreme hopes of Christianity, the hopes which rationalism had released from their dogmatic framework. But for this infusion of Christian fervour, Voltaire's vision of mankind purged of its follies and settling down to cultivate its garden might have come true; and Gibbon's nostalgia for a civilization restored to its antique dispassion might have been satisfied. However, the legacy of Christ blighted these complacent hopes; it had other tasks in store for humanity. So it came that the *philosophes* not only failed to establish an age of quiet enjoyment, but induced instead a violent tide of secular dynamism. And that while this tide was to spread many benefits on humanity, nobler than any that the *philosophes* had ever aimed at, it also degenerated in many places into a fanaticism fiercer than the religious furies which their teachings had appeased. So even before the principles of scientific rationalism had been fully formulated, Rousseau had conjured up the extrapolation of these principles to the kind of secular fanaticism which was actually to result from them.

And he went further. Having anticipated the passions of the European revolution without himself intending any revolution, he anticipated even its sequel which was never intended—and indeed abhorred—by most of those who were to become its actual agents. He realized that an aggregate of unbridled individuals could form only a totally collectivized political body. For such individuals could be governed only by their own wills and any governmental will formed and justified by them would itself necessarily be unbridled. Such a government could not submit to a superior jurisdiction any conflict arising between itself and its citizens.[1] This argument is the same which led Hobbes to justify an absolutist government on the grounds of an unbridled individualism, and the procedure Rousseau suggested for establishing this absolutism was also the same as postulated by Hobbes. It was construed as a free gift of all individual wills to the will of the sovereign, under the seal of a Social Contract, the sovereign being established in both cases as the sole arbiter of the contract between the citizens and itself.

The congruence between the conclusions derived from an

[1] Rousseau, *Contrat Social I*, ch. VI.

absolute individualism, both by Hobbes who had set out to justify absolutism and Rousseau who hoped to vindicate liberty, testifies to the logical cogency of their argument. It suggests that when revolutions demanding total individual liberty were to lead to the establishment of a collectivist absolutism, these implications were actually at work in the process.

Meanwhile this logic was still only on paper, and even on paper the tyrannical consequences of his position were sometimes vigorously denied by Rousseau himself. The predominant opinion of the Enlightenment certainly opposed both the premises and the conclusions of Rousseau, and continued confidently to pursue the prospects of free and reasonable men in search of individual happiness, under a government to which they would grant only enough power to protect the citizens from encroachments by their fellow citizens and by foreign enemies. The logic of Hobbes and Rousseau was suspended by disregarding the question as to who would arbitrate between the government and the citizens. Fascinated by the examples of British parliamentary government, political philosophy was ready to accept the current maxims of British success. It was not Rousseau but Locke, therefore, whose teachings triumphed in the first revolution, which was to be American and not French. And it was still Locke whose diction prevailed in the Declaration of the Rights of Man at the beginning of the French Revolution.

By that time, however, the secularization of the most active minds of Europe and America had advanced nearly to completion and the rising stream of Christian aspirations, emerging from its shattered dogmatic precincts, was effectively entering the field of public life. The French Revolution and the collateral movements of reform in all the countries of Europe brought to an end a political state common to mankind for a hundred thousand years from the beginnings of human society. All during these immemorial ages—throughout their myriad tribes and numerous civilizations—men had accepted existing custom and law as the foundation of society. There had been great reform, but never before had the deliberate contriving of unlimited social improvement been elevated to a dominant principle. The French Revolution marks the dividing line between the immense expanse of essential static societies and the narrow strip of time over which our modern experience of social dynamism had so far extended.

Little did the great rationalists realize the transformation they were engendering. Voltaire wrote that not all the works of philosophers would cause even as much strife as the quarrel about the length of sleeves to be worn by Franciscan monks had excited. He did not suspect that the spirit of St. Francis himself would enter into the teachings of the philosophers and set the world ablaze with their arguments. And even remoter beyond this horizon lay the fact that rationalism, thus inflamed, would transform the emotional personality of man. Yet this is what followed. Man's consciousness of himself as a sovereign individual evoked that comprehensive movement of thought and feeling now known as romanticism. Of this great and fruitful germination I shall pick out only the strand which leads on from Rousseau's exaltation of uncivilized man who, like Adam and Eve before the Fall, has yet no knowledge of good and evil. The scorn which Rousseau had poured on all existing society presently found vent in his defiant assertion of his own individuality. His *Confessions* were to show a man in the starkness of nature, and that man would be himself, whom no other man resembles. His lowest vices would be exposed and thrown as a gauntlet at the face of the world. The reader shall judge, wrote he, 'whether nature was right in smashing the mould into which she had cast me'.

This is modern immoralism. Rascals had written their lives before and had shamelessly told of their exploits. The wrongdoings which a Benvenuto Cellini or a Boswell related in their memoirs exceed those of Rousseau, and their authors showed no compunction. Yet they were not immoralists. For they did not proclaim their vices to the world in order to denounce the world's hypocrisy, but merely to tell a good story.

When Thucydides acknowledged that national interests overrule moral standards in dealings between city states, he declared this as a bitter truth. Machiavelli reasserted this teaching and expanded it by authorizing the prince to over-ride all moral constraints in consolidating his own power. And later, Machiavellism was to develop into the doctrine of *Staatsraison*, exercising a steady influence on modern rulers and contributing greatly to the formation of modern states. This *Realpolitik* culminated in the writings, actions and achievements of Frederick the Great, but still lacked romantic colour. For it still justified itself as a regrettable necessity.

But romantic dynamism transformed this tight-lipped immorality of princes into the exaltation of nationhood as a law unto itself. The uniqueness of great nations gave them here the right to unlimited development at the expense of their weaker neighbours. This national immoralism developed furthest in Germany and was upheld there with a strong feeling of its own moral superiority over the moralizing statesmen of other countries. This German attitude duplicated on the national scale Rousseau's flaunting of his uniquely vicious nature against a hypocritical society. I shall say more about this later.

Meanwhile, let me make it clear that I am not concerned with the effect of Rousseau's writings on the course of history. Their effect was considerable, but even had his works been overlooked, the fact would remain that a great thinker anticipated in three respects the inherent instability of the rationalist ideal of a secular society. He saw that it implied an unrestrained individualism, demanding absolute freedom and equality far beyond the limits imposed by any existing society. He saw, next, that such absolute sovereignty of individual citizens is conceivable within society only under a popular government, exercising absolute power. And thirdly, he anticipated the ideal of an amoral individualism, asserting the rights of a unique creative personality against the morality of a discredited society. And though the transportation of romantic immoralism on to the national scale was admittedly strange to Rousseau's cosmopolitan outlook, yet this too was largely prefigured by his thought. Now that these implications have proved to be paths of history, the fact that they were discerned at a time when no one had yet thought of them as lines of action, strongly suggests that they were in fact the logical consequences of their antecedents: i.e. of a sceptical rationalism combined with the secularized fervour of Christianity. I do not say that these logical consequences were bound to take effect and I shall show in fact that they have remained unfulfilled in some important areas. But I do suggest that wherever they did come to light during the two centuries after Rousseau, they may be regarded as a manifestation of a logical process which first ran its course in Rousseau's mind.

I have set the scene and introduced the ideas which were to move the past five generations up to the stage which is our own

23

responsibility today. I see the course of these 150 years as the rise of moral passions which, though mostly beneficent, sometimes assumed terrible forms, culminating in the revolutions of the twentieth century. I see the present generation still reeling under the blows of these moral excesses, groping its way back to the original ideals of the eighteenth century. But since they have once collapsed under the weight of their logical implications, can they possibly be restored to guide us once more? This is now the question.

I have said that the situation in which the modern mind finds itself today has emerged in two stages from the mentality of a static society. The first stage was the process of intellectual secularization, spreading the new scientific outlook of the universe and yet evoking no profound emotions and calling for no vast political actions; the second was the dynamic process which released these emotions and actions. At this point the thoughts of philosophers were transformed into ideologies. Ideologies are fighting creeds. They fought against the defenders of the static age and they also fought against each other, as rivals. Those who speak today of the end of ideologies, mean that dynamism has abated and can move men today therefore without commitment to a theoretical fighting creed.

The effectiveness of dynamic political action, carried on with little ideological guidance is illustrated by the development of Britain in the early decades of the nineteenth century. The abolition of slavery, the factory laws, the emancipation of Nonconformists and Catholics, the reform of parliament, the lunacy laws, criminal and penal reform, and the many other humanitarian improvements, for which this period was named the Age of Reform, were promoted by people of widely different persuasions. The reforms had their early roots in the sustained struggle against oppression and social injustice which had already found influential advocates in politics for centuries before the Enlightenment. They were not achieved by a secularized anti-clerical movement, but by ancient political forces, quickened by a new zeal for social improvement. With his theory of British political practice, Montesquieu gave an ideology to France; yet in Britain this theory was never an ideology, but a commentary on established forms of life. No one objected, for example, to the fact that Britain's chief executive was responsible to Parliament and that British judges continued to make case-law, although these proceedings infringed the theoretical division of powers. Such was indeed the fate of all political theory in England: it never became more than a set of maxims, subject to interpretation by customary practice. The genius of Hobbes was disregarded, for his teachings were not consonant with practice. Locke was exalted and the great gaps of his theory ignored, for practice readily filled these gaps.

Thus Britain avoided the self-destructive implications of the Enlightenment of which she was one chief author. Remember David Hume's game of backgammon, to which he turned in disgust over the consequences of his scepticism—it has remained the paradigm of British national life. It preserved down to this day the movement of eighteenth-century humanism. In America the same result was achieved through a passionate veneration for the constitution. Hence Britain, whose pioneering scepticism was feared by French conservatives in the eighteenth century, came in the nineteenth century to be looked upon as old-fashioned by the dynamic intelligentsia of the Continent. I have mentioned already how the German romantics, who denied the relevance of moral standards to the external actions of states, indignantly rejected the moralizing talk of English and American statesmen as stupid or dishonest, or both. But German socialists were equally nonplussed by the religious and moral exhortations of British labour leaders. Continental Marxists kept on discussing the curious backwardness of English and American politics—even as Communists in Albania today are probably wondering how countries like Germany, France and England could fall so far behind the enlightened example of Albania.

There was a similar relationship between England and the Continent also in respect to romantic individualism. Byron had spread the image of the noble romantic immoralist through European literature as far as the Russian steppes. The poet Lenski in Pushkin's *Onegin* (1833) has a portrait of Byron in his remote country house. But England itself got rid of Byron without a trace. The problem of evil, the possibility that evil may be morally superior to good, which affected all nineteenth-century thought on the Continent, was never raised in England. Morley, in his book *On Compromise*, deplores the fact that England's civic genius had restrained the adventures of speculative thought so as to keep them politically innocuous. Had he lived to see our own day, Morley might have felt that England had remained backward only on the road to disaster. Or, perhaps more positively, he would have seen that England—like America—had effectively relaxed the internal contradictions inherent in any Christian or post-Christian society, by gradually humanizing society, while strengthening the affection between fellow citizens for the sake of which they may forgive mutual injustice. Because it was this achievement that has preserved the eighteenth-century framework of thought almost intact in these countries up to this day.

However, in 1789, France broke away and led the world towards a revolutionary consummation of the contradiction inherent in a post-Christian rationalism. The ideology of total revolution is a variant of the derivation of absolutism from absolute individualism. Its argument is simple and has yet to be answered. If society is not a divine institution, it is made by man, and man is free to do with society what he likes. There is then no excuse for having a bad society, and we must make a good one without delay. For this purpose you must take power and you can take power over a bad society only by a revolution; so you must go ahead and make a revolution. Moreover, to achieve a comprehensive improvement of society you need comprehensive powers; so you must regard all resistance to yourself as high treason and must put it down mercilessly.

This logic is alas familiar to us and we can readily identify its more or less complete fulfilment from Robespierre and St. Just to Lenin, Bela Kun, Hitler and Mao Tse-tung. But there is a progression from Robespierre to his successors *which transforms Messianic violence from a means to an end into an aim in itself.* Such is the final position reached by moral passions in their modern embodiments, whether in personal nihilism or in totalitarian violence. I shall call this transformation a process of *moral inversion.*

J. L. Talmon's richly documented account of the ideas which moved the French Revolution and later filled the revolutionary movements up to about 1848 makes us realize the depth of this transformation and supplies already some signs of its beginnings. Here is the language in which Robespierre addressed his followers:

'But it exists, I assure you, pure and sensitive souls; it exists, that sublime and sacred love of humanity, without which a great revolution is but a manifest crime that destroys another crime; that selfishness of men not degraded, which finds its celestial delight in the calm of a pure conscience and the charming spectacle of the public good. You feel it burning at this very moment in your souls; I feel it in my own.'[1]

Yes, it existed, this passion of pure and sensitive souls, this sublime and sacred love of humanity—and it still exists today, only it no longer speaks of itself in these terms. Robespierre's text contains some seeds of the more modern terms, when he speaks of that selfishness ('*egoïsme*') which delights in the public good. This phrase echoes Helvetius' utilitarianism, which would establish the ideals of humanity scientifically, by rooting them in man's desire for pleasure. The next step was to reject humanitarian ideals as such; Bentham contemptuously spoke of natural rights and laws of nature as senseless jargon. 'Utility is the supreme object,' he wrote, 'which comprehends in itself law, virtue, truth and justice.' We have seen that the logic of Bentham's scientific morality was mercifully suspended and its teachings interpreted in support of liberal reforms in England, but on the Continent we see henceforth the scientific formulation of dynamism entering into ever more effective competition with its original emotional manifestations. Both were revolutionary in scope, and the Utopian phantasies of both bordered on insanity; but as time went on all these inordinate hopes became increasingly assimilated to teachings claiming the authority of science. And the new scientific utopianism declared that the future society must submit absolutely to its scientific rulers; once politics has been elevated to the rank of a natural science, liberty of conscience would disappear.[2] The infallibility of Rousseau's general will was transposed into the unassailable conclusions of a scientific sociology.

About the same time, personal immoralism that had issued from Rousseau, underwent a similar scientific incrustation. It resulted in the character first described by Turgenev as a *nihilist*. The line of romantic immoralists which Pushkin had started in Russia with the Byronian figure of Onegin and of Herman (the

---

[1] J. L. Talmon, *The Origin of Totalitarian Democracy*, London (1952) p. 68 (my translation).

[2] See F. A. Hayek, *The Counter-Revolution of Science*, Glencoe, Illinois, (1952), particularly his study of Comte, p. 138 ff.

Napoleon-struck hero of *the Queen of Spades*), was not discontinued. Raskolnikov develops their problems further, by committing a murder only to test the powers of his immorality. The figure of Raskolnikov was independently re-created by Nietzsche in his tragic apologia of the Pale Criminal in Zarathustra, and this figure, with others akin to it, gained popular influence in Germany and France. But not in Russia. The popular ideal of the Russian enlightened youth from about 1860 onwards was the hard, impersonal scientific nihilist, first embodied in Turgenev's hero, the medical student Bazarov.

Men of this type were called 'realists', 'progressives', or simply 'new men'. They were strict materialists, who combined their total denial of genuinely moral ideals with a frenzied hatred of society on account of its immorality. Thus they were morally dedicated to commit any act of treachery, blackmail or cruelty in the service of a programme of universal destruction. On 21 November, 1869, the nihilist leader Nechaev had his follower, the student Ivanov, assassinated in order to strengthen party discipline. This is the story which Dostoievsky has told in *The Possessed*, representing Ivanov by Shatov and Nechaev by Piotr Stepanovich Verkhovensky.

The structure of this crime prefigured the murder of his own followers by Stalin; but there was yet some theoretical support needed. It was supplied by a new scientific sociology claiming to have proved three things: namely (1) that the total destruction of the existing society was the only method for achieving any essential improvement of society; (2) that nothing beyond this act of violence was required, or even to be considered, since it was unscientific to make any plans for the new society, and (3) that no moral restraints must be observed in the revolutionary seizure of power, since (*a*) this process was historically inevitable, and so beyond human control and (*b*) morality, truth, etc., were mere epiphenomena of class interests so that the only scientific meaning of morality, truth, justice, etc., consisted in advancing those class interests which science had proved to be ascendant. Such action would embody all morality, veracity and justice, in the only scientifically acceptable sense.

This scientific sociology was supplied by Marxism-Leninism. Though said to transform socialism from Utopia into a science, its convincing power was due to the satisfaction it gave to the Utopian dreams which it purported to replace. And this proved

28

sufficient. Any factual objection to the theory was repelled as a reactionary attack against socialism, while socialism itself was safe from criticism, since any discussion of it had been condemned as unscientific speculation by Marx. Marxism provides a perfect ideology for a moral dynamism which could express itself only in a naturalistic conception of man; this is its historic function.

The generous passions of our age could now covertly explode inside the engines of a pitiless machinery of violence. The pure and sensitive souls to whom Robespierre had appealed still existed, and were indeed more numerous than ever, and his sublime and sacred love of humanity was still burning as ever. But these sentiments had become *immanent* in policies of *manifest* immorality. Their accents had become scientifically didactic. Listen to an example of Lenin's language in the programmatic statement made in June, 1917:

> The dictatorship of the proletariat is a scientific term stating the class in question and the particular form of state authority, called dictatorship, namely, authority based not on law, not on elections, but directly on the armed force of some portion of the population.

Robespierre's terror had justified itself by its noble aspirations; Marx refused such justification and said that violence alone must be the aim of a scientific socialism. This is moral inversion: a condition in which high moral purpose operates only as the hidden force of an openly declared inhumanity.

In *The Possessed*, the earlier type of *personal* inversion is embodied in Stavrogin, whom the modern *political* immoralist Verkhovensky is vainly trying to draw into his conspiratorial organization. But by the twentieth century the two types become convertible into each other throughout Europe. The personally immoralist bohemian converts his anti-bourgeois protest readily into the social action by welcoming an 'armed bohemian' and thus supporting absolute violence as the only honest mode of political action. The two lines of anti-nomianism meet and mingle in French existentialism. Mme de Beauvoir hails the Marquis de Sade as a great moralist[1] when Sade declares through one of his characters: '. . . I have destroyed everything

---

[1] Simone de Beauvoir, *The Marquis de Sade*, Grove Press, New York, 1953, p. 55. '. . . owing to his headstrong sincerity . . . he deserves to be hailed as a great moralist.'

in my heart that might have interfered with my pleasure.'[1] And this triumph over conscience, as she calls it,[2] is interpreted in terms of her own Marxism: '. . . Sade passionately exposes the bourgeois hoax which consists in erecting class interests into universal (moral) principles.'[3]

I have said before that romanticism recognized the extension of national power as a nation's supreme right and duty. This political immoralism is also a moral inversion, akin to the personal immoralism of the romantic school. Meinecke has shown that German *Realpolitik*, the identification of Might and Right in international relations, was the ultimate outcome of the Hegelian teaching of immanent reason. The strength of immanent morality is proved by the violence of manifest immorality. This, Meinecke thinks, is the grim truth blandly overlooked or hypocritically papered over by moralizing statesmen and English-speaking people in general. He admitted that the knowledge of this truth tended to brutalize its holders, but thought that the English-speaking people had avoided this depravation only by turning a blind eye on the disparity between their teachings and their actions. He could see no honest way out; and I would agree that there is no way out that is not exposed to the suspicion of dishonesty.

A great wave of anti-bourgeois immoralism sweeping through the minds of German youth in the inter-war period, formed the reservoir from which the SA and SS were recruited. They were inspired by the same truculent honesty and passion for moral sacrifice which turned the nihilists of Russia, whether romantic or scientistic, into the *apparatchiks* of Stalinism.

People often speak of Communism or Nazism as a secular religion. But not all fanaticism is religious. The passions of the total revolution and total wars which have devastated our age were not religious but moral. Their morality was inverted and became immanent in brute force because a naturalistic view of man forced them into this manifestation. Once they are immanent, moral motives no longer speak in their own voice, and are no longer accessible to moral arguments; such is the structure of modern nihilistic fanaticism.

Here then is my diagnosis of the pathological morality of our time. What chance is there of remedying this condition?

The healer's art must rely ultimately on the patient's natural

[1] *Ibid.*, p. 54; [2] *Ibid.*, p. 54; [3] *Ibid.*, p. 63.

powers for recovery. We have unmistakable evidence of these powers in our case. From its origins in the French Revolution the great tide of dynamism had been mounting steadily, both spreading its benefits and causing its pathological perversions, during roughly 150 years; and then—at the very centre of revolutionary dynamism—the tide turned. Pasternak dates the change in Russia around 1943. It arose in an upsurge of national feeling. Hatred of Stalin gave way to the resolve of conquering Hitler in spite of Stalin. Victory was in sight, and with this prospect came the growing realization that the existing system of fanatical hatred, lies and cruelties was in fact pointless. Intimations of freedom began to spread. These thoughts repudiated the core of Messianic immoralism and for a moment broke with its magic. A process of sobering had set in. In 1948 Tito defected from Stalin, invoking truth and national dignity as principles superior to party discipline.

The decline of ideological dynamism set in also on this side of the Iron Curtain. In England, in Germany and in Austria, the change of heart was noticeable from the early 1950's. Socialists who, even in notoriously reformist countries like Britain, had demanded a complete transformation of society, began to re-interpret their principle everywhere in terms of piecemeal progress.

Finally, the events following the death of Stalin (1953) clearly revealed that a system based on a total inversion of morality was intrinsically unstable. The first act of Stalin's successors was to release the thirteen doctors of the Kremlin, who had quite recently been sentenced to death on their own confession of murderous attempts against the life of Stalin and other members of the government. This action had a shattering effect on the Party. A young man who at that time was a fervent supporter of Stalinism in Hungary described to me how he felt when the news came through on the wireless. It was as if the motion picture of his whole political development had started running off backwards. If party-truth was now to be refuted by mere bourgeois objectivity, then Stalin's whole fictitious universe would presently dissolve and so the loyalty which sustained this fiction—and was in its turn sustained by it—would be destroyed as well.

The alarm was justified. For it is clear by now that the new masters of the Kremlin had acted as they did, because they

31

believed their position would be safer if they had more of the
truth on their side and less against them. So deciding, they had
acknowledged the power of the truth over the Party and the
existence of an independent ground for opposition against the
Party. And this independent ground—this new Mount Ararat
laid bare by the receding flood of dynamism—was bound to
expand rapidly. For if truth was no longer defined as that which
serves the interests of the Party, neither would art, morality
or justice continue to be so defined, since all these hang closely
together as has eventually become apparent.

So it came to pass that the whole system of moral inversion
broke down in the Hungarian and Polish risings of 1956. These
movements were originally not rebellions against the Communists, but a change of mind of leading Communists. The
Hungarian rising not only started, but went a long way towards
victory, as a mere revulsion of Communist intellectuals from
their own earlier convictions. The first revolutionary event was
the meeting of a literary circle, the Petöfi society, on the thirtieth
of June, 1956. An audience of about six thousand, overflowing
into the streets to which the proceedings were transmitted by
loudspeakers, met for nine hours. Speaker after speaker demanded freedom to write the truth; to write about real people,
real streets and fields, real sentiments and problems; to report
truthfully on current events and on matters of history. In making these demands many speakers were reverting to beliefs they
had previously abhorred and even violently suppressed.

In the months that followed these reborn principles worked
their way rapidly further, frequently bursting out in self-accusa-
tions by Communist intellectuals who repented their previous
connivance in reducing truth, justice and morality, to mere
instruments of the Party.

This is how the decision matured which Gyula Hay, since
then imprisoned by Kadar, declared on 22 September in
Irodalmi Ujsag:

> 'The best Communist writers have resolved—after many diffi-
> culties, serious errors and bitter mental struggles—that in no
> circumstances will they ever write lies again.'

Hay realized that on these grounds all writers, both inside
and outside the Party, were now reunited. In a speech made on
17 September he declared:

'We Hungarian writers, irrespective of party allegiance or philosophic convictions, form hereby a firm alliance for the dissemination of the truth.'

It was this alliance which lent its voice to the hitherto mute and powerless dissatisfaction of the workers. When the students marched into the streets to hold their forbidden demonstration, tens of thousands streamed from the factories to join them. Within hours the army had changed sides, the secret police was dissolved. The heavily armed and severely disciplined organization of a totalitarian state evaporated overnight, because its convictions had been consumed by its own newly awakened conscience.

This upsurge of truth resembled up to a point the Enlightenment of the eighteenth century, but it differed from it profoundly. For the Encyclopaedists were not repudiating a string of lies which they had deliberately swallowed, in order to strengthen their own political convictions. There was no occasion for them to restore a belief in truth and morality, which had never been questioned by the orthodoxy they were attacking, nor ever been scorned by themselves.

By contrast, the process of the Communist revulsion had been dramatically told by the Polish poet Adam Wazyk, himself a Party stalwart, in his *Poem for Adults*, written a year before the events in Hungary started. Fourier had promised that socialism would turn the seas into lemonade, and so the Party members had eagerly swallowed sea water as if it were lemonade. But eventually their stomachs turned and from time to time they had to retire and vomit. The word 'vomiting' has since become a technical term for describing the recoil of morally inverted man: the act by which he violently turns himself right way up. A new term was needed, because nothing of this kind had ever happened before.

The Hungarian Revolution is the paradigm of an intellectual movement which, in less dramatic forms, has spread all through the area of receding dynamism, almost everywhere outside Communist China. The Soviet Government has condemned its manifestation within its own domain as revisionism, and I think the name 'revisionism' may be applied to the different forms of this movement everywhere.

Revisionism recoils from a negation. The negation took place

33

when the Enlightenment, having secularized Christian hopes, destroyed itself by moral inversion; and the recoil from this negation occurred when moral inversion proved unstable in its turn. This recoil is the source of all revisionism.

But, unfortunately, to recognize these antecedents is to call in question all the ideas which have hitherto guided revisionist movements. A re-awakened national feeling has been one of these ideas. Pasternak tells us how it humanized the Soviet régime during the war; it has then served the restoration of humane ideals in Poland, Hungary and Yugoslavia. And perhaps above all, it rejuvenated the ancient societies of Asia and Africa, creating, along with much wasteful strife, new popular communities which transcend the ideological conflicts of European dynamism.

Another revisionist idea lay in the new found alliance between liberalism and religious beliefs. The Churches seemed to recall modern man from a state beyond nihilism to his condition before the secular enlightenment. And finally, the sceptical mood of the Enlightenment itself has been given a new lease of life. The more sober, pragmatist attitude towards public affairs which has spread since 1950 through Britain and America, Germany and Austria, reproduces in its repudiation of ideological strife the attitude of Voltaire and the Encyclopaedists towards religious bigotry.

But revision cannot succeed by merely returning to ideas which have already proved unstable. The rule of a dogmatic authority is no more acceptable today than it was in the days of Voltaire. We shall not go back on the scientific revolution which has secularized extensive domains of knowledge. We shall not go back either on the hopes of Christianity and become as calmly indifferent to social wrongs as secularized antiquity had been. And national feeling has proved in the past no safeguard against the descent of dynamism into moral inversion. In fact, *all the logical antecedents of inversion are present today just as they were before*. Can the very channels which had previously led into moral inversion now offer a retreat from it? Surely not for long.

I do not wish to explore this question much further. We *have* arrived beyond nihilism today, even though the place at which we have arrived is similar to that where we stood before; and we cannot foresee the creative possibilities by which men may discover an avenue which will not lead back to nihilism. But one possibility should be mentioned.

Perhaps the present recoil may be stabilized by the upsurge of a more clear-sighted political conscience. We might conceivably achieve a kind of suspended logic, like that which kept Britain and America so happily back from the road to disaster, and indeed this might come about the way it did in England. The religious wars of Europe reached this country in mid-seventeenth century and strife tore England for many years. One King was beheaded, another deposed. But the settlement of 1688, the Petition of Right, the doctrine of John Locke, put an end to this conflict and established, for the first time since the rise of Christianity, the foundations of secular society. Civility prevailed over religious strife and a society was founded which was dynamic and yet united. May not Europe repeat this feat? May we not learn from the disasters of the past forty years to establish a civic partnership, united in its resolve on continuous reforms—our dynamism restrained by the knowledge that radicalism will throw us back into disaster the moment we try to act out its principles literally?

It may happen. But this is hardly a legitimate field for speculation; for from this point onwards, thought must take on the form of action.

Messianism, Nihilism and the Future
RICHARD LOWENTHAL

T o look for the origin of the nihilistic ideological passions that have devastated the lives of our generation and are still menacing the next; to try to discern the chances for an abatement of these passions, on which the survival of civilized life on our planet may depend—there could hardly be a more important subject for a discussion of the role of ideas in our time.

Yet Polanyi's approach to its analysis, for all its original and fruitful suggestions, seems to me to suffer from two opposite limitations. On one side, he confines his inquiry deliberately to the inner logic of ideas, as if the whole witches' cauldron of our time had been set a-boiling by an initial error in the recipe; in his setting of the scene heresies are breeding further heresies almost without regard to the conditions of life which confronted the heretics. Of course, this is a conscious methodical device; Polanyi shows his awareness of its limitations when referring to the merciful lack of logic displayed in the English failure to follow up the same initial assumptions which elsewhere led to nihilism. But as this example shows, it is most unlikely that a valid forecast of the chances for transcending the age of ideological passions could be made without going beyond the limits of the history and logic of ideas.

On the other hand, and paradoxically, Polanyi does not seem to have taken the ideas whose origin and role he is discussing quite seriously enough. If I understand him rightly, he defines modern nihilism as the cult of revolutionary violence not as a means to an end, but as an aim in itself; and he apparently assumes that this concept covers both Nazism and Stalinism. It is his thesis that the manifest political immoralism of both has developed from a common origin in the passionate social morality of Rousseau by a process of 'moral inversion', because the

37

original moral purpose, having become combined with a 'naturalistic' view of man, ended by becoming 'immanent' in the cult of force. He traces several roads to nihilism, and we meet on them such varied characters as the Marquis de Sade and the German romantics, Nechayev and Nietzsche, Lenin and the French existentialists; but the critical point of 'moral inversion' through which all these roads must pass is located with Karl Marx, who—according to Professor Polanyi—said that 'violence alone must be the aim of a scientific socialism'.

I submit that this interpretation bears no obvious relation to anything Marx ever wrote, and is indeed in demonstrable conflict with much he did write. But if that can be shown, it affects not only Polanyi's map of the historical road to modern nihilism, but his basic concept of the identical ideological origin of the two great 'secular fanaticisms' of our time.

Let me, then, state at the outset that Communist and Nazi *ideological* attitudes to violence have always been sharply different—even during the period of the worst Stalinist crimes. The crimes, of course, were similar; the ideological justifications were not. There was a cult of violence for its own sake, a belief in the value of war and brutality in themselves for raising a higher type of man, in Nazism and Fascism—over and above the belief that violence was needed for victory, as a means to an end. There was no such belief in Stalinism where even the worst crimes were justified as needed for the defence of the threatened 'workers' state' against 'imperialist plots', the most ruthless mass deportations and liquidations as necessary stages towards the attainment of the classless society and the fulfilment of humanistic values.

Lest anybody should think this a distinction without a difference, three of its practical consequences should be mentioned here. The first is the contrast, a hundred times attested, between the callous indifference of the Soviet labour camps and the deliberate sadism of the Nazi KZ's, used as a means for 'hardening' the SS *élite*. The second is the simple fact that we all are alive, though Stalin had atom bombs since 1949; if he had gloried in violence for its own sake and not as a means to an end, to be judged by criteria of expediency, we probably should not be. The third is the very same intellectual revolt of Hungarian and Polish Communist writers which Polanyi describes—a revolt based on the discrepancy between the professed humanistic

38

values and the inhuman practice of the régime: if the ideology had been as 'nihilistic' as the practice, there would have been no revulsion among its believers.

Professor Polanyi is barred from perceiving the difference by his belief that the cult of violence as an aim in itself started with Marx. He bases this view on Marx's criticism of detailed plans for a socialist Utopia, which, according to Polanyi, argued 'that nothing beyond this act of violence' (the revolution) 'was required, or even to be considered, since it was unscientific to make any plans for the new society'. Yet Marx, while rejecting detailed institutional plans, did in fact draw fairly precise outlines for his own Utopia. He wrote of the two post-revolutionary stages of Socialism—public ownership of the means of production, with equal rewards for equal labour—and Communism—abolition of the wage system and distribution according to needs; of the 'withering away' of the state as a separate apparatus of force, once the 'dictatorship of the proletariat' had broken the resistance of the former exploiting classes and destroyed their economic basis; of the disappearance of the structural difference between town and countryside, and of the professional division of labour between supervisory and manual work. Such was the classless society which was to be the final outcome of the proletarian revolution; nor did Marx even regard violence as indispensable for the achievement of this aim in all countries. In his famous speech at Amsterdam on September 8, 1872—immediately after the Hague Congress which had split the first International and ended his participation in it—Marx admitted 'that there exist countries like America, England, and if I knew your institutions better, I would add Holland, where the workers may be able to attain their ends by peaceful means'. By contrast, he believed that violence was needed to achieve these ends in the leading continental countries; but it was the ends that were given by his general theory, and the means that were contingent to him. In turn, these aims were clearly derived from the humanistic values of the enlightenment; and whether these values were based in his mind on a 'naturalistic' view of man may be open to controversy in the light of the philosophical writings of his youth.

Marx and his followers, then, did not refuse to 'justify' revolutionary terror by its 'noble aspirations' any more than Robespierre had done—though the language used by them in defining these aspirations was, of course, different. In attacking 'bourgeois morality' as hypocritical, they never ceased to attack it from the basis of its own professed values—the values of the Judaeo-Christian and liberal-humanist tradition—and to claim that only the destruction of the existing social and political order could lead to a society truly inspired by these values; in just the same way, the revisionist critics of the Stalinist dictatorships in Hungary and Poland attacked its practice as hypocritical on the basis of its own humanistic ideological claims. This attitude is diametrically opposed to that which, starting from disgust with the same hypocrisy of the old order, concludes that the values themselves are false and should be replaced by an honest cult of the right of the stronger, the ennobling qualities of violence and the rejection of all traditional moral restraints in principle. That latter attitude, to which the term of nihilism should properly be reserved, can be traced—in different versions and on different levels—in the Marquis de Sade and in some figures of Dostoievsky, in Nietzsche and the 'social Darwinism' of Spencer and his school, and finally in the Fascist and National Socialist movements. But while it is rooted in a similar historical situation as Jacobin and Marxist political Messianism, and may ultimately lead to similar political consequences, it is a spiritually and ideologically quite distinct phenomenon. This remains true, although there have been notable cases of a confusion of both attitudes, as with Bakunin and Nechayev, and with the discovery of de Sade by Marxist existentialists in France, and of transition from one to the other, as with Mussolini.

Given, then, that the political Messianists of the Left start from the common humanistic heritage of our civilization, what is there in their ideology that has led them repeatedly to erect terror into a system of power? I can discuss here only two elements, the first of which is by now generally familiar: the belief in a secular paradise, and in its dependence on the achievement of total power by an organized *élite*.

Professor Polanyi has pointed to the example of the chiliastic sects of the pre-Reformation and Reformation age, and to the secularization of the Millennial dream with the general secularization of Western society. But in speaking of 'secular fanaticism' and 'moral passions' rather than of secular or political religions he has, I feel, underestimated the power which the revolutionary myth derives from its specifically religious content; the writers who have stressed this aspect—men like Berdyayev, Waldemar Gurian, F. A. Voigt, or Talmon—were themselves religious thinkers, and they knew what they were talking about. There is more than 'moral passion' in an elaborate system that tells us that mankind started in a state of innocence (state of nature, primitive Communism), was corrupted by ambition and avarice (class society, state, exploitation) and will eventually enter a realm of perfect justice where all sin (oppression, exploitation, rivalry) and conflict will disappear and no compulsion will be needed: this is a sacred history and a promise of salvation on earth. Marx's achievement as a mythmaker was precisely to have invested the 'laws of history' and the class struggle of the proletariat with this religious meaning.

Yet the Marxian myth of the inevitable victory of the proletariat that would bring about the classless society was only the basis from which a totalitarian ideology, with all the consequences we know, could develop: it was not yet that ideology itself. For those consequences one further step was required—the unconditional identification of the hope of secular salvation, not with the victory of a class, of a social or historic force, but with the power of a specific organized group and its leader. An abstract paradise may justify crimes—but only a concrete Messiah can authorize and order them.

With Karl Marx, the Messiah remained abstract: the Proletariat. He wrote of its dictatorship, but had no definite views about its necessary political form; Engels even came to regard a democratic republic as the specific form for it towards the end of his life. Marx never led a conspiratorial party or aspired to power in its name, he was a prophet, but it did not occur to him to claim the role of Messiah for himself. More than that, he was convinced that the victory of the proletariat could and would take different political forms in different countries. If his passion was attached to the final aim, his powerful mind and his working energy was devoted to an understanding of all the varied forms of the process that would lead to it: there could be no passepartout, no master-key to history—and *a fortiori* no universal political recipe.

It is this fixation to a recipe of total power which marks the transformation of a chiliastic myth into a totalitarian ideology.

In theory, salvation may still be providentially inevitable, but in practice it comes to depend on the triumph of the true believers, organized in an exclusive sect. This triumph, the conquest and preservation of power by 'the Party', thus comes to be viewed as the one indispensable guarantee for the achievement of the final aim—the precondition for the attainment of all the values which motivated the movement. Power (not violence as such) thus becomes an intermediate (though not an ultimate) aim in itself; the vision of the believers is focused on this single point through which the March of History must pass, and on which all their energies must concentrate, and is correspondingly narrowed. Henceforth, all actions will be judged solely by their expediency in the struggle for power, not by reference to the moral values embodied in the final aim: the intermediate but indispensable aim of power has attracted all the salvational importance of the final aim unto itself, and has come like a dark tunnel between the believer and his original Utopian vision.

In the Marxist tradition, the decisive step in this transformation was accomplished by Lenin. Marx, in contrast to many of the revolutionary conspirators of his time, never accepted the doctrine that 'the end justifies the means' as a general principle. He approved of revolutionary terror against the 'class enemy'—he admired both the Jacobins for using it when in power, and the Russian 'Narodnaya Volya' for using it in opposition to Tsarism when other means were denied them. Yet he was genuinely horrified by Nechayev's 'murder for Party discipline', just as were most Russian revolutionaries at the time: while repudiating what he called 'bourgeois morality', Marx in fact judged the actions of his fellow-revolutionaries by a definite moral standard and not by exclusive reference to the expediency of Party power.

Lenin, on the other hand, did regard every means as justified in principle; it is no accident that he expressed admiration for Nechayev's energy and ruthlessness, though he did not specifically refer to the murder. If he did accept in practice certain restraints in dealing with opponents within his party, even after he was in power, the borderline could not be defined within his doctrines, and Stalin only carried Leninism to its logical conclusion in doing away with those restraints. The basis for the decisive change from Marx to Lenin was, of course, that Lenin's political Messianism was institutionally and personally concrete as Marx's was not: Lenin was convinced from an early date that unless his party took power, the aim could not be achieved, and that his party could not win and hold power unless it followed his leadership.

Yet neither Lenin nor even Stalin ever regarded power as an end in itself: they kept justifying their actions by the vision of the aim, and seeking to transform society at great cost in order to get nearer to it. Still less did a nihilistic cult of violence for its own sake develop at any stage of the moral descent from Marx via Lenin to Stalin. The true horror of Communist political Messianism, unlike that of nihilism of the Nazi type, is the horror of unconscious and indeed fanatical hypocrisy—of ruthless amoralism justified by the subjectively sincere profession of belief in a millennial rule of the saints.

To the Conservative, not only any revolutionary, but any radical critic of the traditional order and its conventional hypocrisy easily appears as a nihilist. Many of the young Russian followers of the critic Pisarev in the late 1850's, for whom Turgenev coined the term, were not even political revolutionaries, though they certainly advanced a crudely naturalistic view of man; they were, in fact, proponents of the new morality of the emancipated Russian intelligentsia, and formed part of a broader intellectual current to which also such revolutionary social critics as Chernyshevsky belonged. In the 70's and 80's, the terrorists of the Narodnaya Volya, to whom the label of nihilists was generally applied in the West though not in Russia and least of all by themselves, were men and women who combined ruthlessness in striking down a few selected enemies with exceptionally high moral standards and with an insistence that they did not wish to use force to secure power for themselves: once they had overthrown Tsarism, they proclaimed, they would call the first free elections in Russian history and compete in them, with an anarcho-socialist programme, on equal terms with any other party. The only documents of the Russian nineteenth-century revolutionary movement that deserve the description of 'nihilist' as used today are some of Bakunin's paeans to the 'creative delight of destruction', and particularly the 'Catechism of the Revolutionary' he wrote for Nechayev; and only these documents, which were sharply rejected by the bulk of the contemporary revolutionaries, show a combination of the cult of destruction and violence with the vision of the anarchistic millennium of free co-operators.

On the whole, however, the believers in the 'creative delight of destruction' have been people who rejected this vision and the underlying Christian and humanistic values. They have rejected both Christian charity and secular fraternity, both the equality of the immortal souls before God and the equality of mortal citizens before the law or in their social status and chances. The millennium that *their* Messiah was to bring was to end the degenerative influence of both the gospel and the enlightenment, and to restore the healthy, revitalizing rule of the strong, of the aristocracy of Nature. The formal structure of their vision of history, it is true, showed the same origin in the tripartite apocalyptic scheme as that of their Marxist antipodes, with biology replacing economics as the master-key to history, the state of innocence identified with racial purity, and the fall with the bastardization of the chosen race; but the content of the final vision and the values inspiring it were so diametrically opposed to Christian morality that there seems to be almost as little point in describing the racist ideology as 'chiliastic' or as a 'political Messianism' as there is in describing the Marxist myth as 'nihilist'.

Yet the apocalyptic form of the racialist myth points to the fact that it, too, represents a secular religion—a sacred history mapping out the road to salvation on this earth. Only its spiritual model is not to be found in the typical chiliastic heresies, but in the antinomian and satanistic ones—those which sought escape from the burden of guilt and moral conflict in the doctrine that every 'sin' was permitted to the Elect, and that the ability to commit deeds which to others were deadly sin without a sense of guilt was the very proof of election. In Norman Cohn's study of medieval heresies which Polanyi quotes, the wide spread of this form of heretical mysticism—the so-called 'Free Spirits' or 'Spiritual Libertines'—in medieval Europe is documented in detail; it also shows that the communities of the Elect, having attained, in their own conviction, a state of union with God or even of independence of God, felt entitled not only to satisfy all their carnal desires but amoralism, based on the overcoming of all moral conflict by the introjection of God, was the sign of salvation; while the persistence of the pangs of conscience was evidence of separation from God, and hence of damnation.

Now it is these 'amoral supermen'—not 'moral supermen', as Polanyi misquotes—whom Norman Cohn describes as the remote precursors of the followers of Bakunin and Nietzsche and of 'the armed bohemians of our days'; he does not assign that role, as Polanyi's text would suggest, to the chiliastic sects confronted by the problem of power (such as the Taborite extremists in the Hussite wars or the Münster Anabaptists during the Reformation), whom he views as the remote precursors of our contemporary Communists.

In the first place, the 'Free Spirit' heresy, like its modern secular counterpart, is not universalist: unlike the true chiliastic sects, it offers a road to salvation not to all mankind, but only to the few who are called to use, and abuse, the many. Further, it is not originally political, in the sense that the salvation of the believers does not depend on a triumph over their adversaries and the achievement of the final state of mankind: once they have individually become Free Spirits, once they have joined the ranks of the Elect, they are God-like and free from sin. It follows that their freedom from all moral restraints does *not* depend on a calculus of political expediency—on the right to use all means for a sacred end—but is absolute, and this applies just as much to modern nihilist *élites*. The otherwise most perceptive analysis of contemporary secular religions in F. A. Voigt's *Unto Caesar* errs in the statement that both the proletariat in the Marxian and the master race in the Hitlerite myth are 'free from sin': the Marxian proletariat is not free from sin, but has the mission to bring about a millennium in which its own proletarian condition will disappear along with all the conditions of human corruption, but the Hitlerite master race is indeed free from sin as such, even before its victory, and therefore absolutely above all moral yardsticks.

There is, then, in Nazism no 'moral inversion' in the sense in which Polanyi uses the term; for the manifest immoralism of its methods of action, so far from being in conflict with the 'master morality' underlying the movement, is its direct, if extreme, manifestation. Rather we may say that there is here—and also in Nietzsche's revolt against Christian values, or in Bakunin's glorification of the brigand as the true revolutionary—a genuine nihilism, a morality of negation: for all these attitudes do not

45

spring from a pagan unconcern with Christian values rooted in a different culture, but from the desperate efforts of people reared in the Christian tradition to throw off the burden of guilt which has become unbearable to them.

I have tried to separate the moral attitudes embodied in the two major secular religious currents of our time, and to indicate their spiritual origins. What of the historic context in which they have gained power over the minds of men?

Before risking any hypothesis about dynamic causes, there are clearly some intellectual conditions, common to both of them, which must be listed. There can be little disagreement about those among students of modern history. The first, emphasized by Polanyi, is secularization itself—Man's attempt to conceive the meaning of life in this world in immanent terms. The second, closely linked to this, but perhaps not fully brought out in his paper, is the democratic concept in the broadest sense of the word: the idea that the political and social order, no longer regarded as God-given, should derive its sanction from the will of the people. It is perhaps not superfluous to point out that all totalitarian ideologies are based on the fiction that the totalitarian movement represents the true will of the people, the *volonté générale* in Rousseau's sense; the fiction is not confined to the totalitarianism of the Left, as J. L. Talmon seems to assume, but was equally used as a justification of Italian Fascism by Giovanni Gentile, its original official philosopher, and in Germany by Karl Schmitt. In fact, of course, the very idea of a totalitarian political movement gaining power and then continuing to mobilize the masses for the purposes of its régime is only conceivable in an age where a democratic legitimation has become indispensable for every régime.

The third major intellectual condition for the rise of the revolutionary historical myths is the conscious experience of historic change, and the fourth the confidence in the scientific predictability of the natural order engendered by the progress of science, which is then extended to the field of history. On both points, there is no need for me to add to Professor Polanyi's paper. Together, secularization, the democratic concept, the experience of historic change and the belief in its scientific predictability form the indispensable intellectual background to the totalitarian ideologies or 'secular religions' we are discussing; but they also form the general intellectual background to the modern world since the end of the eighteenth century. Yet these ideologies have arisen with powerful effect, in certain countries and at certain times, while others have proved largely immune to them.

The logic of secularization, of the new democratic legitimation, and of the belief in the predictable progress of history has thus not been sufficient to produce these ideologies *by itself*; more specific factors must have been decisive for their rise at specific places and times. Perhaps the best way to start the search for these dynamic causes is to begin from Professor Polanyi's reference to the 'merciful lack of logic' of the English. It seems to me that, in seeking an explanation for the comparatively undramatic course that the process of secularization took in England and some other countries, he has overlooked the most obvious common factor in the life of those countries—the role of Protestantism in its post-Calvinist form.

To understand that role, it may be helpful to cast our minds back to an earlier great moral crisis of the West—the crisis that began in the Renaissance and was ended by the Reformation and Counter-Reformation. Western society and the Roman Church had long learned to live with the contradiction between the eschatological morality of the gospel and the corruption of natural man, and had adapted a workaday version of Christian morality which combined the necessary sanctions for social discipline with practical toleration of an irreducible core of sinfulness, acceptable to all but the small chiliastic underground current. But this version was tied to a traditional way of life which became increasingly disrupted with the rise of a commercial economy in the advanced regions of Renaissance Europe, from Flanders to Northern Italy and Bohemia; and as this disruption proceeded, the moral prescriptions of the Church tended to appear increasingly absurd and illogical at the very time when masses of believers, socially uprooted and uncertain about the conduct of their lives in the new conditions, were most in need of its guidance. It was in that moral crisis that chiliastic sectarianism first grew from a scattered underground into a mass movement, and that the worldly corruption of the Church became bitterly offensive to large numbers of believers.

Now this crisis had arisen before the age of secularization,

47

and it was overcome within the framework of Christian belief—
by a number of spiritual and hierarchical changes which ultimately resulted in a revision of the moral code commonly
accepted by Christian communities. The contents of the new
code, based on a new accommodation of Christian values to a
more dynamic and acquisitive society, were not vastly different
in the Calvinist countries of Northwest Europe and the Catholic
countries who had passed through the Counter-Reformation;
but the manner in which the new code was 'enacted' differed
decisively. In the countries of modernized Catholicism, the new
code, like the traditional one before it, continued to depend on
the authority and discipline of the Church; hence its validity in
the minds of the faithful was bound up with the validity of
Christian dogma. In the countries of Calvinism and post-Calvinist sectarianism, Church authority was successively nation-
alized, democratized, splintered and finally broken up in favour
of the autonomy of the individual conscience; yet in the very
process of revolt against the old Church, the new code had been
internalized and embedded in that individual conscience, there
to take on an existence that no longer depended on any external
authority, old or new.

I believe that this difference is the key to the riddle of why the
modern process of secularization and democratization has
affected different Christian communities in so radically different
ways. Where the Christian code of conduct was bound up with
the authority and discipline of the Church, and the Church
closely linked with an authoritarian State, the decline of belief
in dogma, by undermining the authority of both Church and
State, was bound to produce both a political and a moral crisis.
Where morality had ceased to depend on Church authority, the
decline of dogmatic belief produced no moral crisis in the lives
of the people, and political institutions could be revalued as con-
venient rather than sacred. To this day, it is a common experience that the former Catholic who loses his faith may become
either an unbelieving hedonist or a believing Communist, while
the former Puritan, when ceasing to be a believing Christian,
tends to become a secularized Puritan. The post-Calvinist countries—Britain, the United States, Holland, and also the Scandinavian countries where the Lutheran State Church during the
nineteenth century lost much ground to various 'Free Churches'
of the Anglo-Saxon type—have produced no secular religions

because the process of secularization, having failed to undermine the internalized morality of modern Protestantism, created nò void in the lives of their people.

It is not difficult to see how this analysis could be applied also to other Christian and non-Christian communities. Russian orthodoxy was not only authoritarian and closely linked to Tsarist despotism, but had never undergone a reformation or counter-reformation adjusting it to the problems of modern life; hence in nineteenth-century Russia, the moral crisis with which Western Europe coped in the Reformation and the crisis of secularization were telescoped into one, in the sense that the secularization of the intelligentsia's thought faced it with the need to reconstruct its moral and religious attitudes from their very foundations: the void to be filled was larger than anywhere in the West. German Lutheranism, a form of Protestantism whose development was arrested at an early stage, before the working out of a 'modern' code of Christian morality achieved in the Calvinist West, retained a peculiar polarity between obedience to outward authority in all matters of the political and social order, and a personal morality that was internalized in the individual conscience yet remained formless and incalculable: under the impact of secularization and the destruction of traditional authority, it gave rise both to romantic individualism and to a sense of anomaly—a moral void resulting in a craving for leadership. Among the non-Christian religions, it seems logical to expect that those in which both the element of metaphysical dogma and of authoritarian organization are weak, while the moral teaching is central, as in the higher versions of Buddhism, would survive the impact of secularization particularly well; the opposite might be expected of Islam, whose teaching has long been bound up with the traditional social and political order.

The foregoing discussion has suggested what I believe to be one of the dynamic causes—as distinct from the general intellectual preconditions—for the rise of the secular religions of our time: the collapse of traditional authority in a society where rules of conduct are dependent on external authority both for their preservation and their gradual adjustment to changing conditions. Where that happens the conjunction of secularization and social change produces a moral crisis analogous to the

Western crisis of the Renaissance, and out of that crisis arise secular religions which are equally analogous to the openly religious chiliastic and satanistic movements of that earlier period. In either case, it seems to be the unbearable conflict between the experience of the changing world and the teachings of traditional authority, rather than the fact of secularization as such, which produces first the widespread sense of disorientation and uprootedness and then the flight into a new fanatical faith.

At this point, we must return to Professor Polanyi's image of an 'outburst of moral passion', which evidently is his interpretation of the same phenomenon. If I understand him correctly, he would agree that it was the destruction of traditional moral authority that made that outburst possible, and he could also without inconsistency accept the above view that it was the non-authoritarian character of post-Calvinist morality that deprived the process of secularization of similarly catastrophic consequences in the area over which this spontaneous moral conformism of the Nonconformists held away. But where I feel I must part company with him is his idea of 'moral passion' itself —the attempt to explain the fanaticism of the new movements by a sudden increase in the moral sensitivity of man.

The concept of passion properly belongs to the realm of psychology; yet psychology, as Polanyi himself points out, has hitherto not spoken of moral passions, only of instinctive passions and moral restraints upon them. He seems to have overlooked that psychology is thoroughly familiar with the phenomenon of instinctive passions masquerading as moral in order to overcome the restraints. In the compulsive individual, an intense effort to restrain aggressive impulses may lead to an apparent excess of self-sacrificing, altruistic kindness; yet as this extreme of altruism is turned into a moral yardstick for judging his fellows, it enables him in fact to yield to his aggressive impulses under the mask of a censorious saintliness. The Freudians know this classical mechanism of apparent 'moral inversion' as 'the return of the repressed'.

The example of individual psychology suggests that, when confronted with an apparent sudden increase in moral idealism in the history of our society, we should beware of taking it at face value and rather look for conditions that may have produced an intensification of moral conflict, leading to a morally disguised eruption of aggressive tendencies. There seems, in fact, to be little reason to assume that the balance between instinctive passions and restraints has ever substantially changed in the course of the history of civilized humanity, though the concrete nature of permitted instinctive outlets and socially enforced taboos has assumed an infinite variety of cultural forms; and the complaint that Polanyi sets out to refute—that man's morality has failed to keep step with the progress of his power over nature—seems correspondingly meaningless to me. The meaningful complaint, and one that I have heard much more frequently, is that man's understanding and control of the forces active in human society, and hence the adjustment of the concrete content of his morality to the changing nature of that society, has failed so to keep in step; and that cannot be refuted by pointing to the 'outburst of moral passion' which on the contrary, if analysed in its historical context, points to that very failure of adjustment.

In fact, the broadest common denominator for the origin of both the openly religious and the secularized forms of chiliastic or satanistic mass movements appears to be that they arise where civilized societies have failed to respond adequately to accelerated social change—to adjust their institutions and their moral codes to the changed situation in such a way as to preserve the possibility of meaningful life in accordance with their basic values. Wherever technological and social change causes large numbers of people to lose their accepted place in society, shattering both their material security and their sense of their own worth, it also undermines their confidence in the meaning of their way of life and their readiness to abide by accepted rules of conduct. The intense self-doubt, anxiety and frustration of the materially and morally uprooted masses find expression in conflicting tendencies to aggressive rebellion and passive submission—tendencies which may then be canalized into acceptance of a chiliastic or satanistic ideology offered by any disaffected prophetic *élite* that is ready to hand and sufficiently organized for exploiting the crisis. What appears as an outburst of utopian hopes and demands, a sudden insatiable longing for perfect justice on this earth, is really a desperate reaction to the glaring failure of the old order to live up even to its own imperfect traditional standards in a radically changed situation; what appears as a sudden nihilistic rage to throw off all moral restraints is really a desperate flight from intolerable moral conflicts in a world whose accepted codes have become transparently meaningless or hypocritical. The established compromise between the ideals of religious ethics and the incorrigible sinfulness of man, or between social discipline and the instinctive drives of the individual, is not shattered by a sudden increase in either saintly idealism or animal brutality; the anarchic outbursts of both idealism and brutality are only the consequence of the fact that the established compromise has already broken down, because it has not been adjusted in time to the facts of unpremeditated and unforeseen social change.

The above does not only apply to the once-and-for-all process of secularization and of the breakdown of traditional authority with its religious sanctions, but to all those profound social crises which transcend the field of purely institutional change and endanger the continuity of a civilization and its moral values. The crisis of secularization and the transition from a tradition-bound, authoritarian order to modern industrial society clearly forms the background to the Communist revolutions we have seen, and may yet lead to the victory of totalitarian movements in other countries. But the chiliastic outbreaks in the non-secularized Europe of the pre-Reformation and Reformation period on one side, and the nihilistic explosion of Nazism in modern, industrially developed Germany on the other, were closely similar in origin. As the German case proves, the failure of a modern free society to control its own dynamism of social change may make it as vulnerable to a social and moral crisis ending in an ideological, totalitarian revolution as any society founded on traditional authority that is being undermined by secularization.

Starting from the importance of the collapse of traditional authority in countries with authority-bound rules of conduct as one of the dynamic causes for the rise of our contemporary secular religions, we have thus arrived at a more general factor: the failure of adjustment of institutions and values to accelerating social change. I am, of course, far from claiming that this factor could furnish by itself an exhaustive explanation of the phenomenon under discussion; apart from other familiar elements, a more searching investigation of the interaction between the rise of ideologically disaffected *élites* during the often prolonged period of pre-revolutionary gestation and the growth of the mass movement in the actual revolutionary crisis is needed. What has been said here is merely offered as a corrective to the tendency to interpret the rise of these movements merely as the unfolding of the inner logic of the Messianic ideas which are endemic in our Judaeo-Christian civilization—to explain, in fact, the rise of the ideologies in purely ideological terms.

Survivors of a volcanic eruption, engaged in rebuilding their homes and restarting the shattered routine of their lives, are probably apt to reassure each other that the age of eruptions is over, and that their particular volcano, at any rate, is now extinct. Do we really have better evidence than that for congratulating ourselves on the end of the ideological age?

Apart from the devout wish of most of those who have consciously lived through the past few decades to be saved from salvation, and to be allowed to live the rest of their lives in less interesting times, belief in the end of ideologies is usually founded on two sets of facts: the visible exhaustion of ideological interest in the post-war Western world, also and particularly among the young generation; and the apparent indications of an erosion, or at least a routinization, of ideological fervour in post-Stalin Russia. Now it is a familiar historic experience that periods of great revolutionary upheavals are followed by a sense of exhaustion. But while in England the new sense of national unity and the devotion of civic and moral energies to steady evolution which followed the revolutionary settlement of 1688 showed a remarkable longevity, the exhaustion which followed the end of the Napoleonic wars in France did not. The difference, clearly, lay in the quality of the solutions found for the social and moral problems which had caused the revolutionary crisis: without a solution capable both of winning fairly general acceptance and of being gradually adjusted to further social change, temporary exhaustion was clearly not enough to assure a lasting return to civility.

As for the alleged erosion of the official ideology in the Soviet Union, the facts are as yet far from clear. This is not the place to discuss the problems of the basis and functions of ideology under a victorious totalitarian régime; but it should at least be understood that they are entirely different from the role of an ideology of totalitarian revolution in a free society. Having become institutionalized in a monopolistic party dictatorship to which it serves as *legitimation and driving force*, the ideology may continue to bring about both vast domestic transformations and critical international conflicts long after the masses and even large sectors of the privileged bureaucracy have lost faith in it. Western observers have discerned symptoms of ideological erosion in the NEP-Russia of the middle 20's, which was followed by Stalin's forced collectivization; in the Kirov period of internal relaxation in 1934, which was followed by the great blood purge; in the wartime concessions to Russian patriotic and orthodox traditions, which were followed by the Sovietization of Eastern Europe and the ideological revivalism of Zhdanov. The post-Stalin relaxation of ideological 'monolithism' has in fact been followed by another attempt at an ideological revival sponsored by Krushchev; and though there are indications that the new dictator's attempt to avoid a return to Stalinist mass terrorism has made it more difficult for him to enforce ideological conformity, all the evidence goes to show that both he and his principal associates are true believers *and aware of the dependence of their own rule on the maintenance of the doctrine.* This is not to say that totalitarian ideological rule can never end in Russia—only that the eventual victory of ideological agnosticism is not to be expected unless the power of the party is decisively weakened in another crisis of succession.

Professor Polanyi does indeed go beyond the usual thesis of erosion; he suggests that some of the original acts of repudiation of Stalin's heritage by his successors sprang from a genuine moral revulsion against the consequences of 'nihilist' ideological rule, and thus were true forerunners of the revolt of the consciences of Polish and Hungarian Communist intellectuals which grew from these first tentative steps of destalinization. Unfortunately, the facts do not bear out this interpretation. For instance, while Polanyi assumes that the heirs of Stalin repudiated the frame-up against the Kremlin doctors because they thought it better to have truth on their side, it seems a more natural explanation that they did so because the frame-up had been aimed at some of them; more specifically, the repudiation was announced by Beria, but after Beria's fall his ex-colleagues had no compunction in placing responsibility for the original frame-up on him! Again, Krushchev's 'secret speech' was an important step both in freeing his hand for policy changes by destroying the legend of Stalin's infallibility, and in reassuring the leading bureaucratic personnel of party and state that the replacement of 'collective leadership' by Krushchev's one-man rule would not mean a return to Stalin's inner-party terror; but attempts to make the rehabilitation of some of Stalin's victims the starting point for a truthful rewriting of Party history were quickly stopped. Nevertheless Krushchev's disclosures, as well as his recognition that Stalin had been wrong in his dispute with Tito, shook not only Stalin's but Russia's authority in Eastern Europe, as well as that of local Communist leaders who had murdered their comrades as 'Titoists' on Stalin's orders; and on that basis the genuine moral revulsion of the Communist intellectuals became possible in Poland and Hungary. Yet however encouraging this development was in itself, it seems too slender a basis for proclaiming that a general turning-point has been reached in the attraction of totalitarian ideologies in our time, and of Leninist Communism in particular.

Finally, it should not be forgotten that Chinese Communism achieved total domination of a potential Great Power after more than twenty years of civil war in 1949—at a time when, in Polanyi's view, the ideological age was already on its way out—and has shown an unexampled ideological virulence in recent years. More generally, it is a commonplace that many of the causes which have in the past led to the victory of secular religions in countries freshly torn from a static authoritarian tradition into the whirlpool of industrialization and secularization, are now operating in many of the newly emancipated 'undeveloped countries'; and while there is, on the basis of the foregoing analysis, no predestined inevitability that any or all of them must suffer the same fate, there is certainly no *a priori* reason why the danger of such a development should be less in the second half of the twentieth century than in the first.

I confess, then, that I can find no solid grounds for Professor Polanyi's hopeful view that 'at the very centre of the storm, the tide turned', or that, because of the 'revisionist' movement that shook Eastern Europe in 1956, mankind generally 'has arrived at a point beyond nihilism'—either in the advanced free societies now passing through a phase of exhaustion, or in the large part of the world that is actually ruled in accordance with the Messianic ideology of Communism, or in the newly emancipated nations now grappling with the problems of technical, intellectual and moral modernization. Yet I recognize that Polanyi, for all his hopeful generalizations, is far from taking an attitude of easy, passively expectant optimism, and I agree with him in seeing no reason for fatalistic pessimism either. Just as he warns that 'all the logical antecedents of inversion are present today as they were before', so do I, on the basis of my different analysis, conclude that the type of social and moral crisis which has produced the modern secular religions still confronts many countries and may recur in others. But just as he sees a chance that mankind might learn from past disasters and, recoiling from ideological extremism, might 'establish a civic partnership, united in its resolve on continuous reform', so do I believe that those dangerous crises *may* be avoided or surmounted without breaking the continuity of civilization, provided the institutional adjustments and the reformulations of accepted values required by the continuous pressure of technological and social change are undertaken in time.

Yet I do not think that I do Professor Polanyi an injustice if I retain the feeling that there remains between us some difference of emphasis with regard to the nature of the remedy. To him, the paramount need seems to be the conversion of the intellectuals from Utopian extremism to moderation, from blind trust in the abstract logic of theoretical systems to an appreciation of the value of pragmatic reforms achieved by consent. Yet if I try to survey the experience of those societies that have succumbed to Messianic or satanistic ideologies in the recent past and to consider the problems of those that are now threatened by a similar fate, I am less impressed with the role of misguided intellectuals and more with the relentless pressure of the steadily accelerating change in the conditions of life. I cannot forget that at the start of each revolutionary crisis, the extremist intellectuals were a small and politically unimportant minority, and that it was generally the stubbornness of the defenders of traditional rule and the failure of the pragmatic reformers to act with sufficient boldness which gave the extremists first a mass following and finally victory. Hence I am inclined to place the main emphasis in societies freshly emerging from traditional stagnation, and also in advanced societies suffering from institutional instability, on the need for sufficiently rapid constructive changes—political, economic, and in the underdeveloped nations also cultural—to retain the allegiance of the masses to a common system of values. Nor can I believe that the necessary reforms can be achieved by general consent in all circumstances, however acute the crisis; after all, the English settlement of 1688 is known as the 'glorious revolution', and the tradition of continuous reform started from that basis.

Lest the above remarks be thought too close to the sphere of practical policy for a discussion of ideas, I wish to add one final reference to what may be called the moral conditions of continuous, pragmatic reform. I have suggested that one crucial condition for the undramatic course of secularization in the Protestant countries of the West has been that their moral cohesion has been made independent of dogmatic religious authority by the internalization of the moral code. Life did not cease to be meaningful when dogma withered away; the sanctification of the daily round with all its imperfections proved a lasting alternative to the pursuit of the Millennium. But it seems that this spontaneous moral conformity of the Nonconformists has also proved more amenable to further continuous chance in accordance with changing conditions, yet without an abandonment of basic values, than any authoritarian morality known to us. One of the reasons why the export of English parliamentary institutions has often proved powerless to achieve a comparable climate of social discipline and continuous reform is evidently that it could not be accompanied by the simultaneous export of the Protestant tradition. But as human societies, however secularized or enlightened, cannot preserve their cohesion by the operation of rational motivations alone, I wonder whether in any post-authoritarian society immunity against secular religions can be achieved without a cultural revolution that succeeds in establishing some such form of internalized morality. In the long run this may well prove one of the key conditions for the possibility of continuous Progress in Freedom.

Enlightenment and Radicalism
SIDNEY HOOK

THE field of intellectual history is beset by many difficulties.
Primary among them is the extent to which the assumption—inescapable to the very nature of the inquiry—that
history is made or determined by the ideas men hold, is true.
Leaving aside the influence of complex objective factors of the
physical environment, the pattern of historical events seems
clearly to be woven out of the interacting influences of interests,
ideas, and personality. To assign relative weights to these elements is a delicate task. The best grounded historical accounts
have revealed the unplausibility of all monisms even when the
predominance of one or another factor has been established for
a specific period.

The difficulties of intellectual history are compounded when
we attempt to assess the influence of philosophical ideas on
human affairs. Here the temptation to yield to one's own
philosophical prejudices, to use the record as an argument or
evidence for one's own philosophical beliefs is almost overwhelming. But if our investigation is to rise above a disguised
question-begging apologetic and reach conclusions which
appear valid to inquirers of other philosophical persuasions, we
must resist this temptation. In other words, we must regard the
influence of philosophical ideas in history not as a philosophical
problem but as an historical, empirical problem in principle no
different from an inquiry into the effects of the industrial revolution on the movement of population or the causes of the Span-
ish-American war.

It is from this point of view that I propose to examine Professor Polanyi's main thesis in his essay 'Beyond Nihilism'. I
shall then say a few things in defence of the principle of radicalism which according to him threatens 'to throw us back into
disaster' if acted upon.

Sidney Hook

I

As I understand Professor Polanyi, he is asserting two propositions. (1) The influence of the rationalist ideal of a secular society, which we associate with the Enlightenment, in fact led to the monstrous Bolshevik and Nazi Revolutions of the twentieth century. (2) The characteristic doctrines and practices of modern totalitarianism or nihilism are 'logical consequences' of this rationalist ideal, particularly in its naturalist forms.

With respect to the first thesis everything that Professor Polanyi says seems to me to be an illustration of a loose form of the *post hoc, propter hoc* fallacy. I do not find any valid evidence to support the view that the rationalist and universal humanistic ideals of the Enlightenment played any decisive role in the theory and practice of the architects of the Communist and Nazi Revolutions. On the other hand, there is considerable evidence against this view.

Indeed, Professor Polanyi himself confronted by the fact that the ideals of Locke and Bentham, imported into France with such allegedly disastrous consequences, helped in England and the United States to create an unprecedented, humane welfare economy, not even approached by any religious culture of the past, explains this in terms of the moderating effect of existing institutions. Without examining the truth of the specific assertions made on what institutions in England and in the United states prevented 'the self-destructive implications of the Enlightenment' from being realized, such recognition is inadmissible on the part of any point of a view, such as Professor Polanyi's, which ascribes decisive historical importance to philosophical ideas. For it can be argued with equal logic that what explains the difference between the development of Anglo-American liberalism and the development of European totalitarianism is not the presence of the ideals of the Enlightenment which were common, but the different social institutions which in the one case permitted the gradual social reforms to develop which were inherent in the commitment to the ideals of the Enlightenment, and in the other inhibited them, until the obstructive institutions were swept away by revolution. I myself do not believe that this is the whole story, but historically it has much more to be said for it than the view that the ideals of the Enlightenment entailed revolutionary action. It is certainly closer to the findings of those historians and sociologists who have called attention to the existence of authoritarian social structures in Germany and Russia as predisposing factors towards totalitarianism.

Problems of historical causation as they relate to ideas are tangled enough without snarling them still more with speculations about ultimate doctrinal genealogy and influence. Empirically we must begin here with the quest for proximate causes. The best source books of the ideas which influenced the leaders of the Nazi Revolution are still Hitler's *Mein Kampf* and Alfred Rosenberg's *Der Mythos des Zwanzigsten Jahrhunderts.* Hitler's intellectual mentor was neither Hegel, Nietzsche nor Spengler. It was Houston Chamberlain, whose racialist mythology, irrationalism, and mysticism is as far as anyone can get from the ideals of the Enlightenment. To be sure, as Professor Polanyi points out, the Nazi cohorts were imbued with a consuming Messianic passion and zeal. But it was precisely this type of passion and zeal which were suspect in the eyes of the founding fathers of the Enlightenment. This is especially true of Locke, Hume, Voltaire, Bentham and the philosopher-statesmen of the American Republic. They distrusted 'enthusiasm' as the concomitant of religious fanaticism. Rousseau's glorification of feeling was foreign to them, so much so that one of the standard criticisms of the rationalism of the Enlightenment is that the chill fingers of reason stifled the life of the emotions. It was not the martyrs of Christian piety but the legendary figures of Roman republican virtue which figured in these writings of the Enlightenment as models of excellence.

With one proviso, it is just as far-fetched to attribute to the rationalism of the Enlightenment casual influence on the animating ideals of the leaders of the Russian October Revolution. The Bolsheviks came to power by an historical fluke and in flagrant disregard of the principles of traditional Marxism. No one was more surprised than Lenin himself that the Bolsheviks succeeded in remaining in power. In Bolshevik eyes the ideals of the Enlightenment were the expression *par excellence* of the bourgeois and petty-bourgeois spirit and not of an international classless society. The thinking, so to speak, was two intellectual epochs removed from rationalism. To the extent that they were Marxists, they were critical of the unhistorical approach of the Enlightenment, and insisted that what was reasonable in society could only be determined by stages in historical evolution which limited alternative action. To the extent that they were Bolsheviks, they discarded the restraining and moderating sense of traditional Marxism for objective limitation, for the extremist forms of voluntarism. They ruled by fiat and not by reason.

From 1902 on, when Lenin wrote his *Chto Delat* ('What is to be done'), it was quite clear that he had substituted for the whole evolutionary emphasis of Marxism the view that history could be transformed independently of the conditions which were presupposed by Marx, and the continuation of this point of view from Lenin to Krushchev seems to me to indicate the degree to which this departure is marked. Consequently I regard the theoretical leaders of the Bolshevik revolution not so much as the executives of the legacy of the French Revolution or of the Enlightenment of the eighteenth century, as its executioners, so to speak. It was an emphasis upon will, rather than intelligence or reason.

All this aside, it is controvertible that the twist which European socialism under the leadership of German Social Democracy gave to historical materialism, far from encouraging the dynamic and activistic tendencies in Marxism, tamed them, and substituted the inevitability of gradualism for the inevitability of violent revolution. For them the ripeness not the readiness was all—so much so that on occasions conditions were permitted to become so rotten-ripe that the maggots of totalitarianism found a favourable environment to develop. The socialist revisionism of Bernstein in Germany and Jaurès in France stressed the ideals of the Enlightenment not in order to encourage more revolutionary action, but to make the socialist movement aware of its actual reformist practices and to liberate it from its revolutionary phrasemongery which frightened off possible electoral allies. When Socialist Parties were in power in Europe, their error lay not in too much planning but in too little, not in a bold rationality to remake society but in the timed improvisation of a series of holding operations to preserve a chaotic *status quo*.

The chief causes of the Bolshevik and Nazi Revolutions have very little to do with doctrinal beliefs. They are to be found in the First World War and its consequences. Not 1789 but 1914 deserves the title of the Year of the Second Fall of Man.

The Bolsheviks got their opportunity not by invoking the

rationalist ideals of the Enlightenment but by exploiting the hunger of the Russian masses for peace, and the desire of sensitive minds everywhere to liberate the world from the insane folly of a war whose real issues had far more to do with questions of national prestige and economic hegemony than with the issues of democracy and freedom. Looking back at the fateful days in which the names of Lenin and Trotsky were practically unknown outside of small circles in Russia, Kerensky is convinced that his major error was that he did not take Russia out of the war after the Kornilov revolt. The reason that Churchill was unable to strangle Bolshevism in its cradle was that it rallied to its banner in the early years supporters who were unified not by Marxist doctrine or ideology, but only by their opposition to war. In every country where the Communist movement gained a foothold, it began as an anti-war movement. The favourite rationalization of the tender-minded supporters of Communism, when the news of Bolshevik terror seeped through to the West, was that the price of revolution was small compared to the holocaust of another world war which could be avoided only in a socialist world.

Indeed, if the leaders of the international socialist movement had been fired with a touch of the audacity of the great figures of the French Revolutionary movement instead of being caught up in the hysteria of nationalism, they might have succeeded, if not in preventing the First World War, then in shortening it.

There is no agreement among historians on how to weigh the causes of the rise to power of German National Socialism. The inflation and economic depression, resentment at the Treaty of Versailles, the desire of the industrialists to curb Social Democracy and the trade-unions, the Communist theory of social-fascism and collaboration with the Nazis, the failure of the Allies to make the concessions to the Weimar Republic which they subsequently made to Hitler—all played an incomparably greater role than the witches' brew of doctrine—not one of whose elements were new—with which the Nazis intoxicated themselves. The Nazis proudly regarded themselves in a rare moment of truthfulness as 'the counter-revolution' to the ideals of eighteenth-century Enlightenment.

II

I now turn to the second of Professor Polanyi's theses which asserts that the ideals of the Enlightenment are inherently unstable and logically entail the nihilism of totalitarian belief and practice. This assertion resembles the contentions of Toynbee and Maritain that if one does not worship God, one must worship either Stalin or Hitler or some other human being.

There are two initial difficulties in any such position. First, even if there were a *logical* connection between certain philosophical premises and certain conclusions that have a potential bearing on conduct, this relationship alone would be no warrant for asserting that human beings *in fact* are guided by it. This is particularly true if the relationship is exhibited in a complicated chain of reasoning. Men are notoriously slack in their reasoning and have a livelier sense of the uses to which they can put doctrines than of their strict implications. To imagine that they guide themselves in crucial situations by the logic of their premises and assumptions—of which they are often blissfully unaware—is to impute a rationality to them which exceeds the claims of most secular rationalists in history.

Second, as Professor Polanyi uses the word 'rationalism', it is an umbrella term which covers a variety of doctrines and thinkers. If we speak of 'sceptical rationalism' then we must exclude Locke who believed that moral truths were as certain as those of mathematics. If we speak of 'absolute and inalienable rights' then we must exclude Bentham who regarded the language of the Declaration of Independence as 'nonsense on stilts'. If we speak of Voltaire and Hume, then we must exclude the romanticism of Rousseau. Professor Polanyi speaks of all these tendencies and figures as integral to the culture-complex of the Enlightenment despite the fact that in some relevant and important respects they differ more among themselves than some of them do from the early Burke and the later Hegel (whose *Rechtsphilosophie*, for example, borrows heavily from Rousseau). Nowhere does Professor Polanyi give us a clear statement of what he takes the essential doctrines of the Enlightenment to be. In one place he suggests that the rationalism of Voltaire and Gibbon might have fulfilled the hopes of man for a civilized society had they not been blighted by 'Christian fervour'. Does this mean that rationalism was at fault in being too tepid in its critique of Christian fanaticism, too tolerant of the spirit of intolerance? Or does it mean that any doctrine held with a zeal and passion disproportionate to the evidence of experience threatens to unleash the furies of totalitarianism? Then why make the philosophy of the Enlightenment, which sought to instate the self-critical processes of reason or intelligence as the supreme authority of truth in human affairs, and as the supreme arbiter of the inescapable conflicts among human values, the scapegoat of historical disasters like war and revolution which flowed in large part from a refusal to deal intelligently with their social causes?

It is obvious from the foregoing that I see nothing calamitous in returning to the ideals of the Enlightenment—if, indeed, we are returning to them, which, as I read the evidence, is more of a hope than a fact. But whatever the fact, I for one believe we *should* return to the secular rationalism of the Enlightenment. When I say we should 'return', I mean, of course, return with the difference that the growth of knowledge and the perspective of broad experience make to minds capable of learning from the past. We can now distinguish more clearly between what is perennially valid in the approach of eighteenth-century rationalism and its local or aberrant forms.

What we have learned about the logic of modern science, the patterns of scientific methods, and the findings of modern psychology should immunize us against the easy optimism of the past, whose secular forms, we note in passing, never rivalled the stupendous myths with which religion consoled believers. It should enable us to develop those habits of reasonable expectation which are the hall-marks of a mature outlook on man and history. Modern science suggests to us that we do not have to embrace a sterile scepticism because the certainties of absolutism are no longer available to us, that reliable knowledge about human affairs although difficult is obtainable. It suggests that there are always problems, small problems and large problems, but not one great problem to which a final or total solution can be found. It suggests that like scientific inquiry in any field, intelligent social inquiry is a continuous process, and, as in science, that it is easier to agree on the empirical consequences of proposed courses of conduct than on their alleged presuppositions. It suggests that in human affairs history and tradition are inescapably relevant and are at least as important as other technical factors which enter into the costs of innovation.

What we have learned from modern psychology is more vague but just as pertinent. It reinforces the wisdom of relating values and ideals to human interests and of exposing these interests to critical consciousness and the counter claims by which they may be controlled. It suggests that values which are not felt as actual or possible fulfilment of needs can find no purchase in the business of living and run the risk of becoming mealy-mouthed abstractions that conceal our real commitments. Together with all the other social disciplines, it suggests that where there are no shared interests there will be no common values, that the first step in approaching conflicts of interest after laying them bare, is to mediate between them, to correct, modify, invent or discover the social devices or institutional forms by which they can be made viable. It suggests that we be suspicious of our own zeal and selfrighteousness, that we cultivate our powers of imaginative perception in order to see more clearly the human being in the enemy, and to understand that since a sound position may be defended by unsound arguments, we have an obligation to rethink claims which, because of the paltry reasons offered in support of them, we sometimes reject out of hand.

If this approach is taken we may find that we accomplish more by trying to achieve less. But whatever we try to achieve will require more thought, more planning, experiment and controlled improvisation than secular rationalists have attempted in the past. There is no royal road to social justice and social peace because, among other reasons, there are so many occasions on which they conflict. A respect for history does not always enjoin caution upon us. Over-cautious drivers can be just as much of a road hazard as speed demons. Some historical situations have degenerated into chaos because those in a position to act have played it too safe. They have relied more upon the automatic, allegedly self-regulating tendencies of society or upon the happy chance that something will turn up than upon their creative intelligence for which, despite all its limitations, there is no substitute.

As I understand radicalism in social life it is continuous reliance upon the methods of critical intelligence, or of scientific method in its most comprehensive sense, to negotiate conflicts of value in the hope of finding or discovering shared interests that may be equitably enjoyed. Such methods cannot create values, they can only check or test or appraise them in the light of the best available knowledge of their causes and consequences in experience. The fruitfulness of this approach is to be measured not only by its results but by the consequences of alternative approaches. It does not accept Russell's dictum that there is no such thing as an irrational goal or end except one impossible of fulfilment. For when we examine goals or ends in their actual *problematic* context, we shall find that they are never really final or ultimate. They are both ends and means in different contexts. They are, therefore, subject not only to the rationality of the means-end relation but to the rational control of the several compossible ends to which every sane mind is wedded.

We can return to secular rationalism with confidence as a starting-point for fresh advance, subject to the caveats indicated above. Nothing promises to be more helpful in grappling with the problems of a scientific and technological world. Its explicit and implicit ideals still recommend themselves to the reason of free men—the rule of just law nationally and internationally until it acquires world sovereignty, universal and continuous education, the primacy of the individual, not of individual*ism*, in the social process, growth as a qualitative norm of development rather than some fixed, pre-determined end, the refusal to make politics autonomous of morals and morals autonomous of social and economic life. These ideals still retain validity for our own day and time as guides to programme and policy. If we go beyond them, it will be by following the vision they have inspired. If we repudiate them, we once more fling wide open the doors to the furies of nihilism.

Criticism and Discussion

MICHAEL POLANYI: ... *the alternatives before us* ...

I wish to thank Professor Hook very sincerely for his contribution. It offers a complete counterpart to my own suggestions. In my opinion, or interpreted within my framework, his position would be one of suspended logic. Now, since this is my ideal, I can hardly reproach him for upholding it. The taking for granted of all the humanistic and moral limitations which he referred to in his report would probably have exactly the effect which he expects, namely to restore reason to a position which is altogether beneficent in the way it has been beneficent for long periods of rationalist rule in its utilitarian form, and still remains so in many countries. But I still see two alternatives before us: whether to accept that these limitations are inherent in rationalism, or to think that they arise from some other source—from tradition, from patriotism, from religion. If the latter is the case, then rationalism can only be described as a limited anchorage.

Now I will ask a few of our participants who have themselves recently experienced, not only the movement towards totalitarianism but also the revulsion from it, whether they feel that this kind of analysis is relevant or whether they would suggest something else in addition to what has been said.

PAUL IGNOTUS: ... *Irrational rationalists* ...

Our friend Arthur Koestler, in his books *Darkness at Noon* and *The Yogi and the Commissar*, considers the Communist ideology as a sort of rationalism *à outrance*. His Communists are people who trust reason absolutely, in fact, he would perhaps admit, to quite an irrational extent. Perhaps Communists are, in fact, 'irrational rationalists'? I am sure that at the cradle of the French Revolution one can already find rationalism *à outrance* combined with a sort of irrationalism, with passionate sentimentalism and belief in instincts.

As far as Fascism and Nazism had any philosophy at all, they believed in violence, in force, in anything but reason. In the case of Communists, their vision of history was to some extent drawn up on rational lines, but all the slogans they launched, their passionate attacks were always justified on irrational grounds, through heroism, self-sacrifice.

I never understood, for instance, why Communists should think it is a glorious thing to sacrifice one's life, and I agree with Professor Polanyi that there is an irrational, inordinate moral passion behind this pseudo-rational creed.

Now, to turn to Hungarian revisionism. I am a revisionist only in a very old sense, let us say sympathetic to those social-democrats who used to be called revisionists before the First World War; but, as we know, the term was suddenly applied by Krushchev to deviating Communists and I think it mainly applies to them, though one may include among them people who do not come directly from Communist circles.

I just want to tell you this: our revisionist leaders were either politicians or writers. A politician like Imre Nagy thought, up to his last moment, that he was an honest Leninist and he really felt that Lenin had supplied all those elements of humanitarianism for which he stood up against Rakosi and the Russian quislings. I do not think that he would ever have thought of going back on those teachings. It was different with the writers who followed him and were his friends, for instance Tibor Dery. Dery, from his early youth and throughout the whole of his literary career, was a man who really disbelieved all sorts of general ideas. As far as I could see, what attracted him to Communism was its huge ambitions. It was his experience which made him believe (and this to a large extent confirms Professor Polanyi's thesis) that some simple sort of moral truth such as brotherly love, such as decency, couldn't be done away with, and that everything loses its sense if one doesn't observe and respect and try to serve these truths. This feeling was prevalent amongst leading Hungarian revisionists and thus, in spite of all their revolutionary upbringing, there was in them an important element of traditionalism and an inclination to vindicate traditional moral values.

70

Criticism and Discussion

K. A. JELENSKI: ... *a genuine form of Marxism* ...

Is the 'recoil from moral inversion' the main characteristic of Polish revisionism? Before the war, only very few Polish writers or intellectuals were revolutionaries in the sense that Tibor Dery and other Hungarian intellectuals were. The adherence of part of the Polish intelligentsia to Communism occurred after the Communists were brought to power by the advance of the Red Army. They were not revolutionary intellectuals, they were neophytes who accepted the reigning creed, the religion of the Prince. The ambiguity with which they tried to rationalize their adherence is best described in Czeslaw Milosz's book *The Captive Mind*.

The real believers were to be found only among some young intellectuals, who came of age under the Stalinist régime. What they revolted against after Krushchev's secret speech was the régime's hypocrisy. Polish revisionists wanted to restate Marxism in rationalist terms; they were fighting the whole idealistic side of Stalinism—I use idealistic in the Marxist derogatory sense. They wanted to apply rational methods to study reality; their ultimate aim was to achieve a form of 'Workers' Democracy', which they thought possible on the condition of a return to a genuine form of Marxism.

This of course proved impossible because of the conditions in which the political apparatus in a Communist country must keep power concentrated in its own hands.

It is the disillusioned revisionists, who have become in fact social-democrats who come perhaps nearest to Professor Polanyi's analysis of the abatement of ideological dynamism.

FRANCOIS FEJTO: ... *new explosions of the revisionist trend* ...

Today is the second anniversary of the execution of Miklos Gimes and Imre Nagy in Budapest. Now, Miklos Gimes came to Paris in 1955 and it was then that I met him secretly on several occasions. At that time he was prey to fearful doubts; it was before the 20th Congress of the Party; everything he believed in had crumbled beneath his feet and conversation with him was painful. He did not even know what he was going to do and it was only after much hesitation that he decided to return to Hungary. But he did decide to do so and before he left

71

he came to tell me that he felt he had many things to make good, even if it cost him his life. He was ready then, in 1955, to lay down his life in order to open people's eyes to the truth. He thought that during his years of serving Rakosi as diplomatic editor of the official organ of the Party, *Szabad Nep*, he had made so many mistakes, committed so many crimes and sinned so greatly against the Holy Ghost, so to speak, that he had to pay for it. It was in him that I observed how deeply ingrained in certain intellectuals was that moral sense analysed by Professor Polanyi. It was stronger, of course, in those Communists who were Christians and who like Gimes, became Communists after the Second World War, for moral reasons, because they really thought that Communism alone, independently of Russian intervention, could bring about the recovery of a nation so thoroughly corrupted by the Horthy régime and the amoral Fascism of the Nazis.

Among Hungarian intellectuals there are many such men, for whom Communism was not a career but a means of reforming their country. In 1955 and 1956 they were the ones most affected emotionally and their moral faith was much stronger, in reaction to their earlier beliefs and actions, than that of other intellectuals such as the 'populists', in Hungary, who resembled in some ways the earlier Russian *Narodniks*, although the populists were never so deeply committed to the régime. While working with the Communist régime, they always had certain reservations. For example, I think that my friend Ignotus, although he had been in prison and suffered persecution, on being released when the thaw set in in Hungary, remained much more moderate, more cautious and more realistic in his reaction to events than his Communist or ex-Communist colleagues or the revisionists among the leaders of the Authors' Union.

Professor Polanyi's main theory seems to me to be that there is a sort of perverted moral sense in Stalinism and in Communism in general. I think this theory is indisputable and that it would be worthwhile drawing conclusions from it in relation to Marxism, since it is Marxism and Marxism–Leninism which, after the defeat of revisionism, of the revisionist movements, continues to form the minds of young intellectuals in the East, but by the same ideological and mental processes thus providing these elements with new opportunities for new revolts. Some of my friends think of revisionism as a movement conditioned by the period and limited in time. They believe that since its defeat in 1956 its days are numbered and that revisionism has no future in Eastern Europe. I am of the opposite opinion, in which I share the view of the Communists themselves. I think that it is most significant that, one year after the utter defeat of the revisionists as a political movement, the Communist Parties meeting in Moscow should have adopted a resolution in which, after much discussion, they described revisionism as the chief danger to international Communism. And it is even more significant that this directive, namely 'Revisionism, Enemy No. 1' should still be one of the chief subjects of Communist propaganda. You will agree that this gives one pause, when one thinks that on the one hand the main revisionist leaders in Hungary have been executed, while others are in prison and the revisionist movement has no means of expression in Poland, in Hungary or anywhere else. The Communists—that is to say the Chinese, who are the most extreme Communists—think that only Yugoslavs survive among former revisionists. But Yugoslav revisionism is, I think, quite a different matter as it consists in the quarrel between the extremist elements of the international Communist movement and the Yugoslavs. I am convinced that Marxism–Leninism as it is after its victory over revisionism in 1956 has reached an ideological impasse. While it deprives the revisionist elements of any possibility of expression in the press, we constantly see it making considerable concessions, at least on minor points, to the revisionists, and it is my opinion that in a few more years, when young people, students and intellectuals have got over the defeat of 1956, in view of the inertia of Stalinism, the same causes will produce the same effects and we may well see new explosions, of an intellectual kind at least, of the revisionist trend.

HANS KOHN: . . . *a long period of spiritual preparation* . . .

On one point I am in full agreement with Mr. Polanyi, namely in his insistence on the decisive influence of moral factors in all totalitarian movements. I am among those who believe that even in Nazism—not in Hitler, but in Nazi youth—in Fascism and in Communism there is much moral idealism, if of a perverted kind. But above all I would like to support Professor Hook's first point. It seems to me quite impossible for a historian

73

to regard the Enlightenment as responsible for the rise of totalitarianism. On the contrary, it was the decline of the Enlightenment which made Communism and Fascism possible. The Enlightenment means the end of authoritarianism, the end of dogmatism and intolerance. Those are the three essential features of the Enlightenment and in that sense the totalitarian movements are in opposition to it rather than its consequences.

Why have some countries, such as England and Switzerland, been less subject to totalitarianism than, shall we say, Spain, Germany or Russia? Because in Spain, Germany and Russia, the Enlightenment was already being combated and defeated in the eighteenth century; because the Slavophiles in Russia, the Germanophiles in Germany and the reactionaries in Spain opposed the Enlightenment and thereby prepared the ground for the victory of Communism and Fascism, which did not emerge by chance in those countries, but were the outcome of a long period of spiritual preparation on the part of the intellectuals. Here again I agree with Professor Polanyi that the intelligentsia has much to answer for, the intellectuals have a great responsibility, the intellectuals in Germany from as far back as 1812, and in increasing numbers, the intellectuals in Russia, the Slavophiles and others who, by their contempt for Western enlightenment, prepared the ground for the new totalitarian régimes.

MICHAEL POLANYI: . . . *the path to self-destruction* . . .

The point we are discussing is to my mind not whether the Enlightenment was the direct inspiration of Hitler and Lenin. It certainly was not, and I am accordingly in full agreement with the speakers who said so. What I have said was, in short, that the defeat of the Enlightenment was the logical consequence of an inherent weakness—and that is the point on which we must concentrate if we are to think of the future. Enlightenment had indeed lost considerable ground and had already set foot on the path to self-destruction—on the short path that leads from Voltaire to Rousseau and from Rousseau to Auguste Comte, who already foreshadowed the modern tyranny of political theory based on scientific premises. I have not been the first to make this point, but I insist that we must discuss it here if we wish to know where to look for inspiration in the past.

I have said in my essay that I see the present generation

74

looking back to the ideals of the eighteenth century, but that I was not sure whether this looking back would really lead to any sound course of action. And we are here to discover how, with our greater insight, we can help this generation.

SALVADOR DE MADARIAGA: ... *the hypocrisy of the West* ...

I am in agreement with all those who have established the connection between rationalism and irrationalism. We all know that we are only dealing in words and that actual life is made of human beings: irrationalists are apt to be very rational and there is a very odd irrationalism about rationalists. Communism is a religious attitude today and it is very difficult to consider Communism as merely the outcome of rationalistic Enlightenment rooted in the eighteenth century. In my experience, I have found that rationalism has entered into the composition of events that we are now witnessing in a particularly odd way, in that precisely because of its very beauty, its simplicity, its perfection, it has expected too much and has called forth a great deal of frustration. I should have thought that a tremendous lot of the trouble we have suffered particularly in Europe in the last twenty years was due to the terrible frustration caused by the too high hopes that had been put on the League of Nations. I should have thought also that the too high hopes based on the modern state have led to a similar frustration. The biggest frustration of all was of course due to the fact that the biggest revolution of all, the one brought about in Moscow in 1917, had ended in the appalling failure of 1925 and onwards.

A good deal of frustration is also due to the fact that those who remained free, or at least outside the failures of the Bolshevik revolution, have not come up to expectation either. Hypocrisy is, it seems to me, the hallmark of international life in the West, although, it is administered by those who consider themselves as the representatives of rationalism.

Whenever we think of violence, we very naturally are led to imagine it as active violence, but the contemporary world is absolutely saturated by passive violence, that is to say, people who are powerful enough to sit tight on the wrong which they know they have caused. Now, a good deal of this sitting tight on your wrongs is being liquidated, for instance in Africa and, to a certain extent, in Asia. But it isn't altogether got rid of for a number of reasons, one of which is that this issue of nationalism and sovereignty requires a good deal of airing in public in such places as ours where this can be done in a serene sort of way. The trouble is not merely nationalism, which is forcing many Western governments to a position of hypocrisy; the trouble is an insufficient amount of sovereignty. We are all the time reminded that we can only organize the world in a new phase if people give away their sovereignty, while most nations haven't got any sovereignty to give away. I am not merely speaking of such places as Liberia, or Albania, or Panama, or Guatemala, whose sovereignty is practically non-existent; I am speaking of the sovereignty of the United States. Is the United States really sovereign? Are there not in the United States powers that are more powerful than the people of the United States? That is what I want to know, and therefore, since the nations, even within themselves, have not been able to achieve their own self-possession, how could we expect them to behave in international affairs so as to satisfy rationalists? There must be a conflict there, an inner conflict in the nation which is bound to produce all kinds of trouble including hypocrisy.

PIETER GEYL: . . . *our strength must be in self-confidence* . . .

To represent the French Revolution as having brought to an end a political state common to mankind for a hundred thousand years—as Professor Polanyi seems to do—has to my ears a thoroughly unhistoric sound. It was far from being so entirely novel an event, it resulted from slow-working changes, both in social conditions and in ways of thinking, that had gone on for centuries and which were by no means confined to France and it did not effect so complete a change either. The enlightened despots had shown a lot of social dynamism before the French Revolution, and after it there remained a lot of statism, of clinging to old habits, of respect for tradition, of distrust towards reforming rationalism. The sharp dividing line which Polanyi draws between England and France, or even between England and the Continent, is to my mind equally unjustifiable. He remarks that continental Marxists kept on discussing the curious backwardness of British and American politics. But just look at continental socialists long before this beneficent change that Polanyi sees in the fifties. Socialism there could not be simply equated with Marxism, in France I mention Jaurès, a truly democratic idealist, only remember his action in the Dreyfus case, and as for Holland—but let me first quote what Polanyi says about the doctrine in which France, according to him, led the world (except the Anglo-Saxon countries). 'If society is not a divine institution, it is made by man and man is free to do with society as he likes.' Now this is a doctrine that was rejected by a large majority of Dutch public opinion all through the nineteenth century. There were to begin with the parties based on positive Christian creeds, the orthodox Protestants and the Catholics—the present Dutch Government, by the way, mainly rests on those two—but also Thorbecke the great liberal reformer, the author of the Constitution of 1848, admitted exclusively and emphatically the restraints imposed by history. The Dutch Socialist Party altered its programme in 1937 already, in a non-Marxist sense, so much so that I, just back in my own country, after twenty-two years stay in England, seriously thought of joining it. When I did join it, immediately after the Liberation of Holland in May 1945, I explained my decision by describing the party as the last refuge for a Liberal. As for the change of temper and mentality in the Communist world as a result of the debunking of Stalin and of the Hungarian rebellion, I am not sure that Professor Polanyi is not over-optimistic here, and at any rate, when he talks of the change in the East as being in one line with that decline of dynamic ideology in the West that he wants us to believe took place in the last decade, I cannot follow him. I grant him, that a reawakened national feeling had something to do with the restoration of humane ideals in Russia, or with the attempts in that direction, as I should prefer to put it with the changes in Poland and Hungary. But above all, how is it possible to argue as if before the fifties the two situations in Russia and in Western Europe were, I should no doubt unduly assess Professor Polanyi's meaning if I said, identical, but even comparable? How is it possible to write that 'we'—we of the West, Polanyi seems to mean, although perhaps I should read 'we' on both sides of the Iron Curtain—that we have arrived beyond nihilism today, and then to discuss the creative possibilities by which man may discover an avenue which will not lead back to nihilism? Lead back, as if we had ever been there.

The most sober pragmatical attitude towards public affairs, so Professor Polanyi writes, which has spread since 1950 through

England and America, Germany and Austria, reproduces in its repudiation of ideological strife, the attitude of Voltaire and the Encyclopedists towards religious bigotry. I remark in passing that Voltaire and the Encyclopedists displayed in their repudiation a fervour and an animosity which was not always either sober or pragmatical. Becker's striking phrase about the 'heavenly city of the eighteenth-century French philosophers' comes, I should think, nearer to the mark.

It is my conviction that our civilization, full of imperfections, as it no doubt is, was, long before the fifties, and still is, the home, par excellence, of free discussion and independent thought and that we have lived for quite a while and still live under the outside stress of an expansionist and dynamic ideology. Our strength must be before all in self-confidence, which does not mean that we must be blind to our weaknesses; but the moral reserves of democracy are considerable and we must not forget that.

MICHIO TAKEYAMA: ... *the overwhelming modern civilization*

My country—Japan—waged a war that lasted for fourteen years. All the virtues stored up in the course of history were called upon for the purposes of fighting that war, but amid exceptional difficulties everything was corrupted in the end.

The present wave of anti-American feeling, led by the active minority, which suddenly became violent a month ago is not an expression of nationalism; it is prompted by the demand for peace. We are experiencing modern nihilism in the form of national schizophrenia, due to over-rapid, unsystematic modernization of society. People have lost their roots. Modernization began with the slogan 'The Japanese soul, with European technique'. But modernization has sapped the traditional Japanese qualities.

When we consider what is now happening in China, we can say, all the same, that Japan has managed to absorb the overwhelming modern civilization without losing too much of its own nature. To us Japanese it seems as though other Asian and African countries were trying to do at one fell swoop what we took a hundred years to do. One must hope that other countries will gain what we have gained without losing what we have lost. Japan gained its independence and made its ascent in a period of the most barefaced imperialism; whereas nowadays the highly-developed countries are helping the others. Europe and America are ready to help the Asian and African countries. That is noble. I would like them to make sure, as well, that those countries will develop systematically from the spiritual point of view too, looking at the whole problem not only from the angle of historical ideas, but from the psychological angle as well. Psychology plays a very important part in a country during periods of transition. To take an example, propaganda from the nihilistic-radical side is always up-to-date and psychologically captivating; whereas the propaganda from the side of reason is always outdated and unpsychological.

THEODOR LITT: . . . *no country has more important reasons* . . .

What I observed in Germany in the critical years is that so-called irrationalism and rationalism went contrary to their own programme and formed the most amazing alliances. To go back to the days of National Socialism, we saw a characteristic example of the peculiar mixture of these elements among National Socialist youth and students. On the one hand, Mr. Polanyi is certainly right when, among the forerunners of National Socialism, he attributes an important place to Romanticism. There is no doubt that these young people believed that, in some romantic way, in and through them, the best of Germany's past would come to life again. I remember that at the time one of the Nazi leaders published an article entitled 'Back to the primeval forest'. A critic of the Nazis once said that these young men were behaving like cave-men and one of the Nazi spokesmen took this up enthusiastically and said 'Yes, the primeval forest of the cave-man is coming to life in us. We are reawakening man's primitive instincts. We are there to bring instinct into its own as against degenerate intellectualism.' But when it was a matter of transferring this primitive instinct to political life, then all at once it became rationalism of the purest vintage. And they were convinced that these original impulses could be led to decisive victory in the context of a rationalistic social order, without ever pausing to wonder whether by contact with these rationalistic principles the original instincts would not be to some extent distorted or even lost.

On the other hand, I have been long enough in the East zone

to have seen the early beginnings of Communism there and to have observed that the spokesmen on the German side, whose desire it was gradually to bring mankind to a state of perfection, were convinced that once one had embarked on the Communist way of life and adopted the Communist economy it was absolutely certain to lead to a classless society and bring back Paradise on earth. But when one examined the basic motives of these men, it was simply an innate belief in what was given out as scientific fact. It is quite true that Communism owes its success to the fact that on the one hand it claims to be based on scientific premises and on the other it is capable of arousing fanatical enthusiasm in the breasts of those who wish to make it a reality.

And so once again we have a combination of rational argument and irrational faith which make up the essential strength of Communism. Of course, when we Germans of today look at the situation as a whole and compare our experience, in the East zone at least, of both kinds of totalitarian systems, we naturally wonder what present-day Germany has learnt from this experience and whether it is desirous or capable of building a new social order. It is my impression that two widely-held beliefs stand in the way of a truly democratic society. There are those who would have us believe that, as regards freedom, the difference between the Soviet-occupied zone and the Federal Republic is only one of degree. They say that in fact freedom is restricted in both places in different ways and that careful scrutiny would show that in the West too people are cheated of their freedom by various means, such as the press and the radio, just as they are in the East by the police and propaganda. But that means that people fail to realize that our democracy has at least the overriding advantage of allowing free expression of opinion, even if it is sometimes wrong. Among the opponents of our Western democracy there are indeed many who do not reflect for one instant that they themselves enjoy the privilege of being able to speak up as loud as they like without fearing any unfortunate consequences. I do not think that people realize enough that freedom and democracy are still at home with us in the West. Then there are the others—and this is a most dangerous attitude which I have heard exists also in other Western countries—there are the others who ask what is the point of making all this fuss about freedom. We have it already and we take it for granted.

Totalitarian systems such as Communism take a determinist view of history. They are convinced that progress will bring the world inevitably to the final goal of classless society. If we think of the extensive influence that the determinist concept of science has on the whole of our existence and of the certainty with which people claim that everything in our spiritual life, in society, government and history is determined as precisely as the processes of what we call nature, then we realize how rightly Mr. Polanyi, in his essay on the two cultures, points out that as long as the scientific concept of man is as widespread as it still is with us and clearly is on the other side, the individual will not awaken to his responsibilities in relation to history and to his social environment. I must also agree with Mr. Polanyi when he points out the need to mobilize moral forces in the defence of democratic freedom. Speaking from my own experience in Germany, I would say that no country has more important reasons than Germany to impress on the minds of the rising generation how important a free democratic régime is in the general pattern of human life. As Germans we have an educational task to accomplish of which nobody can relieve us and in which we are sincerely grateful for all the help other countries can give us.

PART II
Prospects for a New Civility

A Rehabilitation of Nationalism?

HERBERT LÜTHY

NATIONALISM belongs to those political concepts which are at once impractical and indispensable. All discussions on nationalism in general are marked by the proliferous and glittering sterility characteristic of discussions of undefined and indefinable subjects, such as those on the spiritual archetypes as defined in C. G. Jung's psychology, both unlimited in numbers and indescribable in essentials, but the muffled existence of which, in the unconscious appears to be evident. This comparison is not arbitrary, for we, also, are dealing with the shadowy realm of collective psychology, which eludes rational consciousness. Every attempted definition of 'the nation', 'the nationalist idea' or 'national feeling' ends in mysticism or mystification; it can only be expressed in images and symbols—flags, myths, totem animals, folklore, cults, rites —representing a sense of belonging to one collective body of individuals essentially different from individuals of any other collective body which is rationally inexpressible. From the nationalist point of view the nation is the embodiment of a higher order 'directly linked with God', with its own soul, will, consciousness and mission, and of which the essence is incomprehensible to all other peoples, or, also, in psychological inversion, one's own nation is the 'universal' or 'humanity's nation', all other peoples being barbarians or sub-human, i.e. the anomaly sets itself up as the sole norm. (With certain typical differences this was the pattern of both French and German nationalism, and one would not have to dig very deeply to find similar claims in other forms of nationalism.) Nationalism is not a generic term; we may analyse one form of nationalism in all its conscious concepts and manifestations and yet not learn the least thing about other kinds of nationalism, all and each of which claim to be radically different from all others, and unique.

If we attempt to formulate a generally valid definition of nationalism, we are left with nothing but a series of negations: the denial of universalism, the denial of human equality, and of the human ratio.

It appears that conceptually, nationalism can only stand for the more or less complete and exclusive adherence to one nation. Historically, however—and particularly in contemporary history—the process is the reverse; nationalism creates the nation. A traditionally constituted population group only becomes a nation when it is converted to nationalism. This, reduced to its barest statement, is a well-known fact. The many fruitless attempts made during the past 150 years to find general and objective evidence of what could be described as forming a nation—language, culture, customs, traditions, history (i.e. conscious concepts) or else biological and territorial unity (i.e. blood and soil)—have in the end invariably led to the final definition that a nation came into being through its national consciousness, i.e. not by way of any particular ascertainable quality, but through a claim which in the final resort rests on an irrational basis. The fact that in the nineteenth century the term 'nation' was applied only to certain European peoples was founded on a historical postulate—only these peoples had a history of their own and national consciousness could only arise on the basis of such a history; the rest of the world's population were 'without history' and therefore 'without consciousness'. In the dawn of European nationalism, when those nations that belonged to the German and Italian cultures, following the example of the older national states of Western Europe also formed themselves into national states, and others, like Greece, Hungary, Poland, which had never gone under completely, were fighting for their independence, the name of 'nation' was like a title of ennoblement belonging to certain privileged peoples, who possessed their own literature, traditions and history, and it then seemed unthinkable that national consciousness could develop everywhere, *ad libitum*. Today, this concept of 'peoples without a history', incapable of developing any national consciousness, has collapsed; all human groups have a history and if some of them were unaware of the fact, European colonists gave them a practical demonstration of it. The history of the Congo is at least as old and varied as that of Belgium, although the Congo started to produce nationalists and historians at a later date. (Every nationalist is a historian, even if he be only an historical story-teller, retelling legends of a golden past.) We can record the 'democratization' of the concept of nationalism ('Nationalism for everyman') during more than a century, via Eastern Europe and the Balkans to the Near East, to Asia and Africa, just as, from the sociological point of view, we can record the democratization of the aristocratic forms of address 'Sir' and 'Madam'; it is just as natural that today the inhabitants of the Congo territories should wish to be addressed as a nation as that they should desire individually to be addressed as Monsieur or Madame, and this is not so much the expression of 'otherness' as a claim to equality. The triumph of nationalism is at one and the same time the triumph of a formula and the final exhaustion of a concept, and because today this concept, 'a nation', has lost all distinctive meaning, we can just as easily declare at the breakfast-table that the heyday of nationalism is over, and at supper-time, that the unremitting advance of nationalism is the hall-mark of our period; both these statements can be supported by extensive dossiers and weighty arguments. Is the form of address, 'Monsieur' or 'Madame', towards porters and washer-women a triumph of the aristocratic principle or a sign of its collapse? I do not ask this question jokingly, and I would take great care not to answer it lightheartedly.

During the past century we have become so familiar with the problems involved in this 'nationalism for everyone' that it is superfluous to dwell on them in greater detail. The perfect nation, comprising the unity of a territory with natural frontiers, language, religion, customs, culture, economic and political viability and social homogeneity, exists nowhere and has never existed, although the nations of Western Europe came relatively close to this ideal picture—the nations of a privileged part of the world in which, during a thousand years, no major invasions or migrations disrupted or intermingled their various peoples, in whose more or less homogeneous societies the idea of the 'perfect nation' could in consequence arise. Everywhere else—as was already evident in Central Europe—nationalism was compelled to master certain offshoots of the national character on which to build its claims to national independence; either a linguistic group, a separate religious tradition, a folklorist peculiarity, or some other special status, even a sociological antipathy towards neighbouring groups, were sufficient as a basis on which to build a nationalistic movement. But in order to become a sovereign nation a group thus constituted was obliged subsequently to acquire what it still lacked, namely the characteristics of the perfect nation—its own particular culture and past tradition, if not its own language (such as the resuscitation of half-dead or long forgotten languages or else the artificial construction of dialects into forms of literary language); its 'natural' territory or such as could from the military or economic points of view become self-supporting, and last, but not least, the psychological unity (*Gleichschaltung der Seelen*) by means of which the national symbols and myths could become effective, and in striving for these ends such nationalism blindly outraged all the evidence provided by geography, world economics, reason, history, and human co-existence. The tragedy of Eastern Europe taught us the law of reproduction by means of which nationalisms, like infusoria, propagate themselves by splitting, and the parallel law of the multiplication of the problem of minorities, due to the multiplication of national states, only to be solved in the end by mass deportation, which did not first appear in European history at the end of the second World War, but after the dissolution of the Turkish Empire. A dozen nationalist movements arose against Austria-Hungary, as many against Turkey, as many against the Russian state; then, following victory or collapse, Croat nationalism against the new Great Serbia, Slovak against Czechoslovakia, Ukrainian against Poland, Transylvanian and Bessarabian against greater Roumania, Macedonian against all the established national states of the Balkans, always with the constant backing of those Great Powers interested in the mobilization of a fifth column; the naïve or cynical zeal with which all the warring powers in the First World War supported every nationalistic or irredentist movement in the enemy's camp was the prelude to the catastrophes that occurred between the two wars.

In one and the same corner of the world today the various nationalist movements sprawl over and through one another and demand, as an expression of their rival claims to power and leadership, the loyalty and enthusiasm of the same populations. We have long been familiar with Arab nationalism, but also with the Egyptian, Iraqi, Druse and Kurd varieties. African nationalism is an undeniable fact, but so also are the Cameroon and the Bamileke, the Ghanaian and the Ashanti, the Congolese and the Lumumba, each of which also bears within itself both the possibility of inner fragmentation and of great-power imperialism. Indian nationalism is established but has to assert itself over two hundred potential nationalisms; the Pakistani has to make itself independent in the face of the Indian, but the Bengalis are still uncertain whether their nationalism is Pakistan or Bengali, and in North Baluchistan Pushtu nationalism is demanding its own Pushtunistan. This list could easily be lengthened; there is no criterion of international law or political philosophy which can prevent any piece of the human mosaic, any sheikhdom on the pirate coasts, any African tribe or clan, any administrative district, once artificially cut from the map by a colonial power, from declaring itself a nation when circumstances and the external balance of power are favourable.

This is no cheap satire on the condition of peoples who, as the result of the decline of empires or the instability of artificially created states, were left without genuine moral or political affiliations. But it is sufficient reason at last to strip the process of nationalization of all romance and mysticism, and to investigate its real functions. A nation does not arise from the instinctive action of a native soul, nor through the free decision of the collective will. We know today that nationalism, i.e. the founding of a nation, postulates nothing else but the existence of a group that can in some way be enclosed within definite frontiers, in whose name a leadership—magnates, knezes, chiefs, priests, teachers, propagandists, cheer-leaders, a native intelligentsia, or a local dynasty—can claim the right of self-determination, i.e. the right to rule over it themselves. Frontiers in this sense may be organizational, administrative, or even merely propagandist; the common link a family or tribal basis, or else a community united by religion, language, or no more than tradition, a Mafia, or, simply, as in the new African states, an artificial administrative unit imposed by foreign rule a few decades earlier. Where such structural elements exist, there also exists a corresponding local leadership, based either on a feudal or religious ruling caste or a native intelligentsia. We tend today to assume that in the development of national revolutionary movements the chief role is assignable to the intelligentsia or semi-intelligentsia, which always and everywhere claims the natural right to governmental and administrative posts, and sees in every aspect of 'non-national' administration both material disadvantages and a personal offence to its racial consciousness. But in Africa today, as in Eastern Europe yesterday, older traditions and also dynastic claims are involved; Sekou Touré, descendant of a race of Sudanese conquerors, and Modibo Keita, heir to the medieval Mali dynasty, have returned, via the *Quartier Latin*, to claim their ancient rights. No section of humanity is without traditions and historically founded claims on which some form of nationalism can be erected; the unfortunate fact is, rather, that the soil of every continent is soaked in historically based titles and claims. Nothing is more ridiculous than to challenge the historical validity of a nationalist movement that has begun to develop, as, for instance, the French have done over Algeria; nationalism, like physical movement, proves its reality by marching on, and even when there had previously been nothing in existence resembling a national consciousness, agitation and struggle can in no time create a tradition and a consciousness and a legitimate claim based on them—for there is no other criterion.

So long as history has existed this process has repeated itself again and again; it is one half of the history of states, of which the other half is the formation of empires. All that is new is the name we have ascribed to it and the ideology that we have attributed to it, namely, 'Nationalism'. When, at the end of the thirteenth century, the members of the lesser nobility and the ringleaders of some Swiss Alpine valleys banded themselves together against Habsburg domination, the sole political claim they laid down in their charter was 'We do not want any foreign judges'. This meant that they desired themselves to exercise the basic function of rulership, the administration of the law, and this claim had the backing of the mountain peasants. It was not a matter of demanding a superior or a better jurisdiction, but their own; not for an improved administration but for self-administration. They preferred even unjust but native judges, acting in conformity with their ancient customs and delivered in the local dialect, to the learned judgements of the Roman law schools delivered by foreign prefects. The basic claim of nationalism is nothing but the basic claim of medieval particularism. When today we refer to the nationalism of the Cameroons or Togoland, we could just as well re-write the history books and be referring to Waldstattian, Appenzellian, Waldausian, Friesian, Albigensian or Novgorodian nationalism. The desire to live according to one's own rights and customs and to be ruled by one's fellow-countrymen is the natural desire of every population group that has developed its own customs and standards of behaviour; the rest is a matter of circumstances, of historical luck, of greater or lesser originality and stubbornness. In the stronghold of the Swiss Alps and Lower Alps, in a corner of Europe where the power politics of the great states were in balance, the medieval particularism to which the concept and ideology of the nation were alien, was able to maintain itself down to modern times; in the greater part of the rest of Europe it was stamped out by the development of absolutist territorial states. It was precisely the chief historical feature of the great nations of Western Europe that as they passed through the melting-pot of absolutism, i.e. the centrally administered state, they were welded out of dozens of particular groups into uniform masses of subjects and these, during the social and political revolutions at the turn of the eighteenth and nineteenth centuries, became nations in the modern sense of the term. For the very reason that they had not developed spontaneously, but were synthetic creations, they needed—or rather, the new leadership that had taken over the dynastic apparatus of government needed—a nationalist ideology to support them.

The concept of the nation, which was equally unnecessary to medieval communal autonomism and to medieval overlordship, belongs historically to the period of transformation at the beginning of the i.. .ustrial age; it was born simultaneously with the twin concept of democracy. The decisive moment occurred with the changeover of the principle of legitimization; when government was no longer carried on in the name of a legitimate rulership but in the name of the people (be it the entire population of the state or its politically active representatives) the population had to be conceived as a political unity. Nationalism was the ideological integrator of the democratic state. An individualistic democracy, such as was dreamed of by the rationalist political philosophers of the eighteenth century, cannot provide a practical form of government, but merely that anarchistic form of Utopia which heads the beginning of every revolutionary movement. (The formula 'Government of the people, for the people, and by the people' postulates the identity of people and state, i.e. the abolition of the state as a separate institution, in the same way as does Marxist theory.) Rousseau, although very much against his wish, knew this to be the case, because he knew the endless civic strifes of the citizens of his native Geneva. Rousseau's entire works are a protest of Genevese-Calvinist reaction against the corrupting penetration of 'frivolous French civilization'—a corrupt local oligarchy supported by France, the introduction of French theatrical companies enforced on Geneva by diplomatic and military coercion —and his reaction was so strong precisely because he himself was a strayed sheep who never found his way back to the fold. A community of subjects requires no national loyalties and an army no patriotic enthusiasm, but a democracy needs a nationalistic ideology for the integration of its citizens and its citizen armies; the French Revolution became nationalistic at the moment when it became terroristic. The nationalism of the nineteenth century was no longer instinctively inborn, but a deliberately fostered ideology of unity. Since the French Revolution all democratic constitutions elaborated a mass of rites and institutions for the training of national feelings—presentation of colours, civic oaths, national holidays, re-writing of history, folklore, the entire apparatus of education and cultural administration was drawn into the service of national consciousness.

Nationalism is basically a terroristic ideology that imposes conformity of thought and behaviour on the members of those population groups it has either seized or claimed. Enmity, suspicion, or prejudice towards other national groups or unassimilated minorities are front-line weapons in the service of nationalist integration. Helvetius said that in a nation of hunchbacks it is a citizen's duty to wear the national hump, i.e. to think, feel and react in conformity to the national basis; nothing is more typical of this kind of ideology than expressions such as 'un-German', 'un-American', etc., which brand the failure to wear the national hump as monstrous or even delinquent behaviour. Autonomism, individualism, or cosmopolitanism, any form of non-nationalistic, pre-nationalistic or super-nationalistic loyalties is regarded in the last resort as criminal. For over a century the cherishing of the nationalist hump and the attempt to condition in the Pavlov manner nationalistic behaviour patterns was the supreme educational aim of school-teaching and the re-writing of history from the patriotic point of view, and with enormous success. Wherever nationalistic ideologies hold power, witch-hunting can at any moment break out; in times of crisis or war every form of nonconformity becomes high treason, and in this century the citizens of all European nations have experienced how effectively this mental terrorism can exclude or defame any form of rational thought.

As nationalism is, according to definition, a national attitude, it is difficult to agree on how it should be defined, and this might lead to a misunderstanding in our discussion owing to the different shades of linguistic meaning between the Continental and the English uses of the term. I fear that I may here be speaking of an entirely different concept from Professor Polanyi's. The advantages of that political good sense he attributes to the English nation, in my opinion, include the fact that they do not know what 'nationalism' ('Nationalismus') is. As far as I am aware, the term 'nationalism' is generally used in English as a synonym for patriotism or love of one's own homeland, and everything that is a matter of public property or public concern is called 'national'; the mystical terminology of nationalism ('Nationalismus') is foreign to a language which refers to 'this country' or 'Her Majesty's Government' whilst elsewhere oaths of allegiance are taken to the fatherland or the nation. The gullibility with regard to such phenomena as national socialism or Arab nationalism which for a long time prevailed in England was largely due to this ignorance of pathological nationalism. I would like to ascribe this very sympathetic but sometimes dangerous unawareness of certain diseases, as is the case with so many other English advantages, to English insularity. I know how silly such distinctions of 'national minds' generally are; but this is a question of language and the meaning of political language in every country is the outcome of that country's particular historical experience and tradition, which makes it more difficult to translate and more subject to becoming absurd in literal translation, than any other. The English were favoured insofar as they were able to become a nation (or to achieve nationhood) without too ardent struggles towards that end, and without having become a problem to themselves in the process of defining 'uniqueness'. Since 1066 the unity of the English kingdom has never been challenged from within or without; there were epic struggles for succession rights and forms of government but not over the unity of succession and government. No Armada since 1066 ever reached the English coast; and even the unification of the British Isles was eventually accomplished as an 'internal affair', without more effective foreign intervention than some important French intrigues in Scotland and Ireland. If the French Revolution had taken place in as similarly privileged circumstances as the English civil war of the seventeenth century and the long subsequent dynastic troubles, and if it had been allowed to develop equally undisturbed by exterior influences, it too might have been spared the transformation into a form of terroristic nationalism. The English citizen, insofar as he did not belong to the aristocracy, was sufficiently protected against foreign influence by the mere insularity of his country, without the necessity for an ideology of nationalistic integration. Until recent times Britain could feel herself sufficiently protected by her fleet to dispense with conscription and any form of militarism along Continental lines, this most compulsory form of 'integration of the souls'; the English are the only people in the world who even today still proudly refer to themselves as subjects, for to be a British subject meant always the contrary of being tied to the soil—an unparalleled liberty of movement over seas and continents—and was a greater privilege than to be a state citizen of any republic.

To be sure, England has developed aspects of nationalism and imperialism just as repulsive as those revealed by any Continental nation, but without posing similar problems; her nationalism remained a form of arrogant insularity and her imperialism was a struggle of a nation of traders and seafarers for the freedom of the seas—their freedom to trade, sail and settle everywhere—not for frontier provinces and frontier populations. During centuries England strove to solve her own nationality problem, the Irish, by every means of suppression, even to genocide, by methods comparable to the very worst Continental examples, but even this remained an internal affair. The history of Ireland is as tragic as that of Poland, but in contrast to Poland Ireland had no other neighbour but England, which lay like a mighty barrier between that small island and Europe; no other Power was able to employ this potential fifth column, no 'world conscience' built up a literature of accusation against the 'enslavers of Eire', no European Lord Byron sang of the sorrows of Ireland; England did not solve her Irish problem any more successfully than France her Algerian, but Ireland never succeeded in becoming a painful spot in world politics. It is not a denigration of these English virtues of 'suspended logic' if I believe that they rest to a great degree on an enviable lack of hopelessly entangled problems and an equally enviable good conscience.

That is probably the reason why the English example, 'often imitated but never attained', has remained so sterile, in spite of all the willingness to learn from it on the part of Continental Europeans; the English constitution is as inimitable as English history itself. Nowhere outside England was 'national unity' a natural condition, to be regarded as a matter of course; everywhere else the ideology of nationalistic integration was indispensable to the foundation of the nation. Some loose form of conditional loyalty is insufficient to hold together a political community that is not merely a collection of subjects; this requires a certain degree of automatic, unconditional loyalty, and where this cannot be postulated in advance, it must be drilled in. When the New England colonies seceded from England their leaders did not concern themselves with the question as to whether their claim to independence was legitimized by their being a nation of their own; their practical, technical motives for rebellion against the legislation of a distant Parliament, that regarded their particular needs and aspirations as of secondary importance, seemed to them amply sufficient for the purpose.

The term 'nationalism' is as inadequate to describe the revolt of the thirteen colonies as it is to describe the revolt of the free Swiss valleys or that of the Mau Mau. American nationalism was subsequently developed, in part very deliberately, as an ideology of integration, as a negation of all those nationalities that went into the 'melting-pot'. But similarly to its English counterpart, free of external problems, this political and rational form of nationalism—the absorption, individually, of displaced persons into a new community, replacing all the national backgrounds from which they originated—is inimitable and untransmittable; the same process has never been repeated elsewhere. The assumption that nationalism and democracy are inseparable—and even practically identical—became a basic tenet of American political thought (e.g. Professor W. MacDougall's *The American Nation*). With Wilson this tenet became a matter of world history, and the least one can say is that it has not helped to make the world safe for democracy. Anglo-Saxon theorists never seemed to grasp the fact that in the old world nationalism was the extreme example of the destructive effect of 'secularized religiosity' and of 'powerful moral passion' that had been led astray, or, if they did so, regarded this merely as the result of occasional and therefore abnormal excesses.

Above all the most deeprooted characteristic of nationalism in settled populations living side by side or sometimes even inter-mingled with one another, which caused not only Marxists but also liberals of the classical school invariably to repudiate nationalism as a reactionary ideology, remained completely alien to both English and American experience; this charac-teristic was the mobilization of the atavistic instincts of an autar-kical agrarian society against the 'uprooting' and 'social disin-tegration' inseparable from modern industrial society. To the same degree as industrialization and world economics dissolved the former links with clan and soil, ancestry, totem animals, the native ground, 'blood and soil', ancestor worship, xenophobia and endogamy became the ideological postulates of nationalism, taught with religious zeal. And in fact nationalism did often serve as an ideological bulwark against revolutionary tendencies, against those of a democratic character in the nineteenth century and against Communistic advances in the twenti-eth (the nationality principle against world revolution, Ver-sailles against Bolshevism, Wilson against Lenin). This bulwark was illusory, and the Bolshevik politicians soon discovered that in almost every part of the world nationalism could in fact be utilized far more effectively as dynamite than as cement: nationalism as an atavistic defence mechanism against the social transformations of modern times—which basically are a defeudalization of humanity—turns for that reason first against the industrial powers of the West, because it was they who had entrapped all other countries into the net of world economy, and because, in the name of free enterprise, they neglected for too long the social consequences of this process (in their own countries as well as in the rest of the world), whilst Communism offered a universal recipe for social reintegration. The attempt of the Western world, made for the first time in Eastern Europe and other border countries of Russia after 1918, to whip up their nationalist ideologies against the revolution, was an admission that they possessed no organizational prin-ciples appropriate to the industrial age, and that they were attempting to exorcize the problems of the present by means of the fetishes of the past; this, in spite of occasional tactical successes was a rearguard battle lost in advance. Today the Western world is beginning slowly and unwillingly to feel its way towards both pluralistic and supra-national forms of organization. There is as yet no indication of a definite success in this direction, yet it is my firm conviction that no other method has any future, and that retreat would be catastrophic.

In recent years Titoism, the East German rising of 1953, the Hungarian and Polish revolutions of 1956, the Tibetan rising and similar events have led to a kind of rehabilitation of nationalism in Western thought. This is in the first instance merely an expression of relief at the fact that the Soviet system is also having trouble with nationalistic reactions, and of the understandable sympathy with every form of resistance to an equally brutal and deceitful despotism. Yet I nevertheless consider it important that we should not develop a double-mindedness with regard to a pathological phenomenon which, when it appears in the West, we regard as a plague, but of which, when it breaks out in the Communist Empire, we approve simply because it causes disquiet to the Communist rulers behind the Iron Curtain. If we were technicians and tacticians of the Cold War, for whom—on the model of Machiavellism in any given period—everything that is damaging to one's opponents is justifiable, we might also include nationalistic ideology among our intellectual weapons, but in that case we would do well to do so with the same degree of cold cynicism with which Communistic propaganda includes nationalism in its own strategy; regarding it as a factor in collective psychology which one must take into account and which can be used as a destructive force against the enemy, but which must be rejected as a means of any constructive policy.

It is indisputable and basically inevitable that the disturbances in the satellite states included a strong nationalistic element. No collective resistance to a strongly grounded overlordship could dispense with an organizational basis, a frame and a symbol of unity. In the Asian, African (and one hundred and fifty years ago, American) colonial territories, the struggle for independence was at first inevitably organized within this colonial framework, even when the latter was a completely artificial and arbitrary creation (and it is clear that in Africa, at least, this is merely a preliminary phase, which must be followed by

97

regional federations or territorial re-organizations of the Black Continent if Africa is not to become 'balkanized' in its turn). In the same way the resistance against the centralized rule in the Soviet Empire finds its natural support in the formerly independent states, which continue to exist as political, administrative and even economic units and which, in their national sections of the ruling party, even possess a certain degree of formal autonomy. Beyond all nationalistic mythology there are purely practical and mechanical reasons why tendencies towards the loosening and differentiation of the Communist bloc must run along such lines, and it is equally obvious that in these cases many historical memories and symbols of earlier struggles for independence should be re-awakened. But these former symbols and memories are also present in our own minds, and we have fallen into the fatal habit of classing every struggle for self-government and autonomy as a nationalist movement, without troubling to investigate its basic motives and claims.

I do not in the least dispute the strength or justification of specifically national effects, or of those rooted in national traditions (the fact, for example, that Poland and Hungary are the two Catholic provinces of Eastern Europe, whose religious tradition for nearly a thousand years was almost identical with their national one, which, among other reasons, caused them to remain immune to the influences of Great Russian, Pan-Slavic and Greek Orthodox propaganda, although it is debatable whether 'national' is an adequate description of such complex historical facts). But the demand for autonomy by cultural, religious, or even simply regional communities, for individual freedom of thought and behaviour permitting individuals as well as historical and social groups to breathe and develop freely, is not in essence nationalistic. The demand of Hungarian workers to have the right to form free trade unions or the struggle of Hungarian peasants against collectivization, do not seem to me to require any additional legitimization on the grounds of national traditions going back to the Hungarian feudal state which knew neither trade unions nor free peasants; and the demand of Hungarian writers for the right to 'write the truth' would only diminish if it were made in the name of a specifically Hungarian truth or national 'otherness'. The demand for human rights and human dignity—which also includes the right to individualism and autonomy of the social groups which make up the human mosaic—is not a national right and needs no nationalistic justification. No doubt we have to reckon with present day linguistics, which define any autonomist movement as nationalism, but in that case we must also draw the consequences of such a misuse of the term. 'Nationalism for everyone' cannot be regarded as synonymous with the traditional conception of the nation as the highest form of human integration, of 'national sovereignty' as the highest organizational form of human relationships, nor with an international order which would be exclusively a system of relationships between sovereign national states, for in this case 'nationalism for everyone' would mean the return of humanity to tribalism and the prehistoric horde. Europe not only provided the world with the concept of the nation, but also with the concept of balkanization. The path to progress beyond the universal totalitarian state and beyond nihilism cannot be sought in a return to balkanization.

Revolutionary Nationalism

ALBERT HOURANI

I F most communities in the modern world have followed the
path of the French Revolution rather than English reform,
that is not because they preferred the doctrines of Rousseau
to those of Locke on intellectual or aesthetic grounds, but
because the experience of France has been more relevant to their
problems than that of England; and it was the gravity of these
problems, rather than the influence of Dostoievsky, which
pushed some of them to the logical extreme of nihilism, while
others managed to achieve the 'suspended logic' of England and
America. Faced with certain problems, all traditional institutions and all habits of compromise, however deeply rooted,
break down. In what follows I shall try to describe some of the
factors which pushed the peoples of the world along the path of
revolutionary secular nationalism; my examples will be drawn
from one group of peoples, those which formerly belonged to
the Ottoman Empire, but what I say may be, in some measure,
relevant to others as well.

That they belonged to the Ottoman Empire is indeed the first
thing which should seize our attention. When the modern civilization of Europe first presented itself to the peoples of the
world, it found most of them in the throes of one of the great
natural movements of history, and indeed the influence of
Europe was first felt as something inserted into that movement
and complicating it rather than as an independent factor. This
movement was that of the disintegration of great empires—
Turkish and Persian, Mogul and Chinese. All these were centuries old, and were undergoing that process by which the
effort of will which creates an Empire relaxes, and the 'charm'
which holds it together begins to fade. The dissolution of a great,
ancient and complex political system brings with it not administrative and economic strain alone but moral strain also. Empires

establish themselves in the heart; to survive four hundred years they cannot rest on force alone but must win themselves a general acquiescence and some active loyalty. So it was with the Ottoman Empire. It was not in its great days simply an autocracy holding down unwilling peoples. That is what it became at the very end, but its becoming so was itself a sign of its decline and imminent collapse. In its great days Ottoman rule had been deeply rooted in its subjects' minds. For the Moslem element (whether Turk or not) the Sultan was the greatest ruler of Sunni Islam, the defender of the frontier against Christian Europe and Shi'i Persia and guardian of the holy cities; between him and them ran the link of the Law, recognized by both as sovereign in the Empire and standing above the ruler's will. The non-Moslem subjects did not look at the Sultan's rule in this way, but they too acquiesced because of economic interest, because of their recognized status as separate communities managing their own affairs under their own lords, or because of that 'charm' which power exercises as long as it is not challenged and while it has not lost its nerve.

When Empires disintegrate they do so in two ways: first geographically, by the escape of regions and peoples from central control into autonomy and independence; secondly, by way of moral dissolution, the relaxation of the bond of trust between government and ruled. The Ottoman Government failed to give its subjects just and efficient rule springing from some principle they could accept, and they in their turn—one section after another—ceased to give it the active loyalty and participation which governments require, in the modern age more than before. This moral collapse was one of which the Ottomans themselves were aware, and even in the great sixteenth century, Turkish writers were analysing the Empire's decay and asserting that there was no remedy except a revival of the public virtues among rulers and ruled. In the nineteenth century the Ottoman Government made a deliberate attempt to bring about such a revival, by creating a new political system which could once more be the focus of loyalty and the ground of virtue. But it failed in the end to create a morally unified 'Ottoman' nation, and there were many reasons for the failure—the chain-reaction set up by the first successful revolt, that of the Greeks; the factor of religious difference, the desire for religious autonomy taking the secularized form of the demand for communal independence; above all, the fact that political systems do not disintegrate easily, and the Empire was forced, in its last dreadful phase, to turn its back on its own ideal of egalitarian patriotism, and become an autocracy simply to survive. Finally, the ruling element itself, the Turks, turned against the Empire as having been more trouble than it was worth, and, in a last scene not without its pathos, declared that the Ottoman Sultanate had 'passed for ever into history'.

With the weakening of the Sultan's power, and still more when he disappeared, a new problem presented itself to all his subjects, but particularly to those who, by education and in other ways, had become conscious of a world beyond their tribe or village. It was not simply the problem of making other arrangements for their administration, for that, over a large part of the Empire, was taken over by Britain and France. It was something more fundamental: a problem of identity. 'Who am I' is the first of all questions; posed in political terms, it could be easily answered during the great Ottoman days. 'I' was a member of a religious community and a subject of the Sultan. But now that the religious community was being secularized and the Sultan's grip had relaxed, it became a real question. It was an urgent one, because a man's self-identification is the basis of his rights and duties, and the moral ground of the community; and it was a complex one, because it was not clear and obvious how men should think of themselves. Brought up in an Empire where races, languages and religions had mixed together, open to doctrines from Europe as well as their own cultures, enclosed in a hierarchy of communities stretching outwards from the family, through tribe, village and district, trade-guild, town-quarter and city to the universal religious community, they could identify themselves in more than one way; and it was only gradually, and not without pain, that the 'nation', defined in terms of an equivocal blend of religion and language, emerged as the basis of political morality and organization.

The new dynamic nationalism, therefore, meant for the peoples of the Near East—and *mutatis mutandis* for other peoples —an attempt to rediscover themselves, to identify themselves and so re-create their political life. It was dynamic and revolutionary, because before life could be re-created it was—or at least it seemed—necessary to shake oneself free from the dying body of the Empire, and also for another reason as well. The vast expansion of Western Europe, and above all of Britain and France—an expansion of goods, of armies, of ideas and political systems—was the greatest event of the nineteenth century, and not only in economic and political history but in that of the human imagination. This inexorable advance, which seemed likely to leave no corner of the world untouched, revealed the existence of a strength as yet undreamed of; and it was clear that the advance could not be resisted, nor European control once imposed thrown off, unless a similar strength could be generated. Thus there began that typical movement of the period, the search for the 'secret' of European strength; and it is characteristic of the difference between that age and this that we, if we posed the question, would think first of all of heavy industry and technology, and the scientific attitude which makes them possible, while our fathers would have tended to ignore or minimize the difference of material strength and lay all their emphasis on the superior political institutions and morality of Europe: on national unity and self-sacrifice, on the active co-operation of governments and people, on representative institutions as a means to both these, and behind all this on the incessant energy—moral, intellectual and practical alike—of the Western peoples. Thus the desire to emulate the strength of Europe seemed to confirm the lesson of Ottoman decline: what was needed was a revival of communal strength and virtue, focused on the idea of the nation, and aiming in the first instance at the overthrow of European control, by violent means if necessary, and then at the re-creation of real political life.

The need for an identity and a community, for public virtue and national strength, the idea of the national as the focus of virtue and Parliamentary government as its school: these are the forces which have led, in the last hundred years, to the partition of the great Empires into several dozen sovereign states. But has humanity in the end obtained what it sought? It is difficult to draw up a judgment on a whole period of history, although equally difficult, and in the end more dangerous, to refuse to judge and believe that history transcends our judgment and is indeed the norm of our morality. But if we had to draw up a balance-sheet for the period of national struggle and independence, it might read somewhat as follows. First of all, the effort to become independent has in fact generated a dynamic energy, a sense of unity and a corporate self-confidence which to some extent have formed the ground of political virtue: nationalism has created a sense of active responsibility, if only for a limited society, and that 'mutual affection of fellow-citizens' of which Polanyi speaks. The care of a national government for its own people, when it exists, is something different from the care of a benevolent foreign government; and the spirit in which men accept injustice from those they regard as belonging to themselves is quite different from that in which they acquiesce in the injustice of a conqueror. But on the other hand, often the moral unity does not go very deep. Much depends on how independence is achieved: if too easily, the process does not produce a real and lasting national cohesion, and if too difficult the cohesion may be created and then broken in pieces. Much depends too on when independence is achieved: it can come too early or too late. Again, the State when created may not be co-terminous with the 'nation' as nationalism defines it, and neither may correspond to the natural community created by geography and history. For all three to have the same extension, there must be a combination of factors such as rarely occurs: clear natural frontiers, one religion, one language and culture, a historical tradition of unity. When this combination is lacking, there is something artificial or abstract about the idea of the 'nation'. Men are defined in terms of less than their whole selves, and the result is a lack of depth and reality in the sense of solidarity, the break-up of historical communities, self-division, and conflicting claims to land or to men's allegiance.

What may be more dangerous still, the struggle for independence has often led to the exaltation of one set of virtues at the expense of others: of those which are necessary for the struggle—unity, loyalty, self-sacrifice—rather than those of the solitary seeker after the truth, or of the kind of citizen or leader who is more concerned to defend the individual against society than to defend his society against another. The national ideal, as moulded by the heroic struggle for freedom, does not always serve as the ground of the moral qualities which are necessary to run a democratic system in an independent State. Once independence has been achieved, Parliamentary government may mean a weak executive and national division; so it is condemned in the name of the national ideal, the complex of ideas built around the concept of the nation tends to dissolve, and the dynamism it has generated finds no channel through which to express itself. In some countries, the resulting frustration may express itself in the attempt to expand; but on the other hand prudence, the euphoria of independence, the consciousness of military weakness, the existence of the United Nations, the influence of the universal principles in the name of which independence has been won—all these may work in the opposite direction. States, being independent centres of decision, must always find it difficult to live side by side, and there can never be a complete harmony of interest between them. The process of dividing the world into sovereign States could not have taken place without friction, and has left behind it, now that it is nearing completion, several million refugees; but it has left behind it surprisingly few territorial disputes. There are only one or two such disputes so bitter that they may lead to a major war; the most dangerous of course is the dispute over Palestine. On the whole, the frustration which comes so easily after independence tends to show itself in moral disintegration: this expresses itself in civil strife or in a civic indifference which leads in its turn to despotism.

The classical nationalism does not always therefore create a lasting strength; but strength—albeit of a rather different sort— is even more necessary after independence than before. The new States find themselves faced with the interests and pressure of the Great Powers, and also with neighbours who, although no Great Powers in the strict sense, may still be great in proportion to them. What is more important, they are touched by new ideas —by that new ideology of economic and social development which is taking the place of the ideology of nationalism, or else giving it a new content. It is only through economic develop- ment, the modern world believes, that nations can be strong and morally united; only a developing State can be morally healthy and united. So the problem is still that of strength, and of the social and political virtues which are inseparably connected with strength. But the type of strength which is needed, and the type of virtue exalted, have changed in the process. If one asks what is needed by a developing society, the answer must be complex: technical accomplishment and the intellectual habits underlying it; political consciousness, the awareness of what is being aimed at; a special kind of social discipline, that of the intelligent individual, con- scious of his own interests but willing to accept subordination of his good to that of others, and of present to future goods;

flexible institutions, free from the chains of custom; a strong executive, able to plan, to impose its conception of change, to intervene actively in the economic process, and to bring about rapidly changes which otherwise might take several generations.

There are some countries, like India and Tunisia, where the ideas of development and reform were implicit in the idea of nationalism even before independence came, and where the social and moral preparation for development therefore took place at the same time as the struggle for independence. In these fortunate countries, it may be that development will come about and the new type of strength be generated within a Parliamentary system, and it is possible to hope for that 'suspended logic', that acceptance of existing institutions, which Polanyi calls for. In other States, however, we must at least ask the question, whether there is not a certain contradiction between Polanyi's ideal State and the kind of State visited by rapid development. The States of Asia and Africa, faced with the need for rapid social and economic change, may well decide that only two paths lie open to them. One is that of Communism, on the Chinese rather than the Russian model, for the example of China—its problems and its sudden leap forward into the age of industry and technology—seems more relevant to Asia and Africa than that of Russia, a European state in a different phase of change. The other is that of 'popular nationalism', with Egypt as the most obvious example: a nationalism which emphasizes the future rather than the past, the heroic individual remaking the social world, the popular will embodied in a popular leader, and a territorial patriotism with the great dams and steelworks as its totems. The dangers of this are obvious. Once more, the dynamism generated by internal construction and hope of better things may be diverted outwards; and the claim for a viable unit of development, for water, minerals or oil-royalties, can give rise to conflicts no less than the claim for 'natural frontiers' or the incorporation of one nation in one State. Once more, the emphasis on the future good of all may lead to neglect of the present rights of the individual. But it seems more likely than not that, except in a few favoured countries, men will be willing to incur these dangers, and for the sake of a real or imagined social well-being, will continue to accept 'the rationalist ideal of a secular society', and to pour into it all the fervour of a religion restated in secular terms.

Criticism and Discussion

HERBERT LÜTHY: *. . . these States have become too small . . .*

I shall deal with only one aspect of the problem—that is, with the question of whether the reawakening of national consciousness in Europe is to be reckoned as one of the phenomena of revisionism that might lead us back, beyond ideological religions, to a peaceful, tolerant and well-balanced society. There are two sets of events that might lead us to conclude that this is so. One of them is our unequivocal approval of the efforts made by the former colonial peoples to achieve independence. This involves the very difficult question of whether that movement should be regarded as nationalistic: in point of fact we are no longer clear as to what really constitutes nationalism, once we get outside Europe.

In my opinion it is completely arbitrary to apply the words 'nationalism' to every movement towards independence by a colonial population, when we cannot even say definitely to what extent it is related to a specific nation. There is no rule of international law, or even of political philosophy, which would justify opposition to the efforts of the Luluas or the Balubas to achieve their independence, or deny them the right to represent themselves as a nation. Neither is there any rule of international law or political philosophy under which we could dispute the right of the Bakongo to pursue the reunification of the sections of their people which have been divided up between the former French Equatorial Africa, the former Belgian Congo, and Portuguese Angola, in the same way that Germany aspires towards reunification. I think it would lead us into great complications if we were to raise the question of the definition of a nation here; and broadly speaking, the international vocabulary has universally adopted the custom of applying the word 'nation' to any community that constitutes a State or wishes to constitute one and, on the strength of that fact, applies for representation in the

109

United Nations. It is almost inevitable for us here in Europe to approach a discussion of nationalism predominantly in relation to ourselves and our own experience, for we are really the only people who have any idea of what the term originally signified.

But to come back to the one point with which I have to deal—does the reawakening of nationalism in the Communist sphere of influence represent a movement towards freedom, one which has important implications for the future? We must of course begin by dismissing the suggestion that all the totalitarian ideologies might justifiably be regarded as equal. For the notion that nationalism, the reawakening of nationalist movements, could ever have helped to overthrow a Fascist or Nazi form of totalitarianism must, of course, be dismissed as absurd. National Socialism, Fascism, the Iron Guard were themselves nationalist movements, out to overcome the Communist danger: we have had that already, and had its results too.

It is a different matter, of course, in the Communist sphere of influence, and we can all make the comparison between the Polish and Hungarian independence movements and those of the colonial peoples. Yesterday we listened to a number of representatives of Hungary and Poland; and it struck me right away as curious that not one of them stressed, or even mentioned, the national aspect of their respective revolutions. The spiritual leaders of those uprisings were concerned, not with a specifically Hungarian or Polish social order, but with a proper form of society. It goes without saying that the struggle had a national flavour about it, because no actual historical struggle can take place in a no-man's-land of abstract humanity; it must be carried on in the actual existing framework of State institutions, with the possibilities they offer for seizing power and fighting political battles. The question is, whether the nationalistic flavour of the battle is its determining aspect, the one which will most influence the future. I have said that it is not, and I deliberately exaggerated the polemical aspect of my paper, because I think it was in the interest of the debate for me to do so.

I would like to present the problem of nationalism as part of the question of a possible international order of society. It was repeatedly said here that the real Fall, the starting-point of the St. Vitus' dance of ideologies and of totalitarian movements, was not the logical result of a particular philosophy or set of deas, but the outcome of the First World War. And the First

World War was not the collapse of a particular social order—bourgeois or capitalist, democratic or totalitarian—it was the collapse of an international order that knew of no principle of organization except nationalism—that possessed no statesmen capable of thinking on an international scale. And the real question I want to ask in speaking of nationalism is whether, even for us, nationalism is still the only conceivable principle of integration. For in the course of history nationalism has served as the principle of integration for the European community, which transcended its small particularisms and individualist features and built up a sense of homogeneity. The nationalism of the great nationalist powers in Europe was not a spontaneous development among people of a national feeling that had existed from the first; it was a deliberately-propagated sense of union, intended to promote the sense of integration, in connection with the transfer of the principle of legitimacy from the absolute ruler to the nation, which became the new principle of unity. By yesterday's standards, though not by those of today, those great powers were too large to generate a spontaneous feeling of unity. Their nationalism was always a form of artificial, synthetic, ideological cohesion, backed up by all the State institutions, including the schools. By today's standards, on the universal scale these States have become too small, and we are confronted by the question of whether or not we can devise a supranational, pluralistic, federalist principle of integration for a supranational order of society which will guarantee the right of every group—not only the existing nations, but every group with individual characteristics—to develop freely.

ALBERT HOURANI: . . . *nationalists directed towards the future*

The modern nation states are our equivalents of the warlords of the past. The form is different because the circumstances are different. You have a spread of education which makes everyone able and eager to help in the political process. You have the loss of the idea of a divine order which the successor can preserve and which gives him his legitimate title to succeed. You have the collapse of the traditional communities into which people can withdraw. The State and its policy matter much more to every individual than they did in the past. And so this process of disintegration has become a conscious one. What was in previous days a struggle of armies has become a struggle of ideas and of parties, a search for a valid principle of cohesion and of legitimacy, a search also for a government or a ruler which embodies it. Now at this point, something arbitrary enters in.

It is at this point that, searching for a principle of legitimacy, people in Asia and Africa took over ideas from Europe. There was something almost accidental about it; but one can trace the process. To take an example in Egyptian nationalism: It was, one can say, almost an accident that one of the first theorists of Egyptian nationalism went to Paris in the first age of European Egyptology. His imagination was touched by the image of ancient Egypt in Paris and not in Cairo. But it is not wholly arbitrary, for what was universal and essential was the sense of European strength. Europe, for Asia and Africa, was to be feared, but also to be admired. And there took place the classical movement of the nineteenth and earliest twentieth centuries: the search for the secret of European strength, which was found in national unity and loyalty. Nationalism, to put it in other words, is the irrational factor, the attractive force which serves to bind people together into a community. Strictly it means nothing except to those who feel it because they are conscious of being members of a community. But we are the prisoners of our own choice. Once adopted, the national idea gathers to itself other ideas, and some of these may be nihilistic ideas: self-worship, assertion of will, the right to expand. But to say this is simply to say that man is sinful, that any belief can be prolonged in a wrong direction: the necessary self-confidence of an imperial people has become the idea of racial inequality. Even liberalism in a nature not strong enough to bear its noble ideals can degenerate into a sort of moral hysteria. Whether nationalism takes this wrong turning depends on innumerable factors: on whether the idea of divine law still exists, whether the judiciary is free, whether the university is free, whether the nation at the beginning of its independent career is fortunate enough to find leaders who possess not only the political power to win independence and to organize it but a genuine moral sensibility, etc.

The world is now divided into nation-states, but a new problem arises, for which the idea of the nation is still essential. The idea of social and economic development involves, as we all know, government intervention over the whole range of life, the active co-operation of people with government, a sense of social responsibility, a willingness to sacrifice present to future goods, and a new relationship between the independent state and the outside world. For all these purposes, cohesion and solidarity and unity are necessary. There must still be some irrational force of attraction which holds together the community. In the modern world, in Asia and Africa, I can see two such forces of attraction: there is the force of the Communist idea and there is the force of popular nationalism. And this popular nationalism is attracting to itself new ideas, any ideas which advance its developments.

One could say, putting it briefly, that the past has been abolished, that the eyes of the nationalists of the present generation are directed not towards the real or supposed glories of the past but towards the future, real or imagined, with the great dams and irrigation works as its symbols. One could say also that the problem of East and West, in its nineteenth-century form, has been abolished: new divisions in the world have been created. You have, then, a new sort of nationalism, a new popular nationalism, dynamic, with its necessities but also with its difficulties and dangers: the danger of conflict, the danger of self-worship and the danger of the denial of the individual in the interest, real or imagined, of social welfare. Again in some circumstances you have the possibility of this idea being pushed to the extreme of nihilism. What are the factors in the modern world, in the new nation-states which incline this new popular nationalism towards the revolution of nihilism and what are the other factors which may make it possible to achieve what Professor Polanyi has called a 'suspended logic', or a 'will to live together'?

HANS KOHN: . . . *the indispensable democratic legitimation* . . .

Professor Lüthy spoke, above all, about the European situation. There Nationalism to a certain extent fulfilled its purpose of acting as a medium of integration whereas in Asia, Africa and in Latin-America today Nationalism provides what might be called 'the Democratic Legitimation indispensable for every government today'. In Asia or Africa or Latin-America, a stable government of any kind is unthinkable today without this 'legitimation'. Only where the existing government—whether it be a 'colonial government', or a traditional government—only where autocracies have not adjusted in time to the changing conditions, nationalism has taken a violent character. On the whole, I would say, from the experience of forty years of study of Asian and Middle-Eastern nationalism that the transition has been much more smoothly done than I would have thought possible. Nationalism is an answer to rapid social and above all psychological transformations in Asia, Africa and Latin-America, and I think that only Nationalism can find there a fairly general acceptance as a means of integration. On the other hand, and there I would agree with Professor Lüthy, the situation in Europe which had come to the very same process 150 years ago is very different. As to Nationalism in the Communist orbit, I would like to recall that when the Russians resisted the German aggression in 1941–2 Stalin did not make any appeal whatsoever to ideas of social justice or Marxism, but purely to what might be called Great Russian Patriotism and called not upon the fighters of the revolution but upon the 'great ancestors', among them Christian saints, feudal princes and czarist generals.

WALTHER HOFER: . . . *in Africa, we have 'independentism'* . . .

I think it is very risky for Mr. Lüthy, in his paper, to reject deliberately, from the start, the idea of any differentiation between what we may call constructive or justifiable nationalism and what the terrorist ideologies call nationalism. All of us agree with what he said about that kind of nationalism. But if we lump together all the historical phenomena that have been connected with the concept of nationalism, I do not think we shall be helping to make history comprehensible; for we shall be bringing into juxtaposition things which in my opinion, even if our ideas of the situation are inadequate, should be kept as far apart as may be. Mr. Kohn has already pointed out—and here I feel sure Mr. Lüthy agrees with us—that there was, after all, a stage of historical development when nationalism did not promote disintegration, when its influence was not destructive—when it contributed to integration by assembling the political rubble of separatism into viable units. I need only mention the nineteenth century, with the examples of Germany, Italy, the

United States of America too, if you like, and on a smaller scale, our common fatherland, the Swiss Confederation, to which Mr. Lüthy, too, makes some references in his paper. Mr. Lüthy said that the world that came to an end in 1914–18 was one which could think only in terms of nationalism. I think another misunderstanding might arise here. In my opinion there has so far been only one period in the history of Europe where the nationalist principle really dominated as far as was possible in the circumstances, and that was the period between the two world wars. Mr. Lüthy rightly mentioned the disastrous consequences of the dismemberment of the Eastern empires—the Austro-Hungarian, the Russian, the Ottoman—and pointed out that the slogan, or principle of the right of peoples to self-determination did not finally lead to any durable order of things. But whether, because of that, we should totally reject that idea, and the attempts it led to, seems to me to be a very different question. I think we should not be too pedagogic in our attitude towards history; I think we should not overlook the fact that the communities established in 1919, and more especially the steady, organized course that certain of them seemed to be following from 1925 onwards, had a very good chance of producing permanent historical effects. Our experience of the Second World War and the utterly pathological, almost unimaginable National Socialist régime in Germany do not entitle us to assume that the statesmen of 1920 should have anticipated such a development—for it lay right outside the framework of European history, even of world history.

Mr. Lüthy very rightly complains, and so do others, that the concept of nationalism seems to have lost all substance nowadays and that it is no longer possible to put forward any positive definition of it. He was right, too, in saying that in the field of international law, 'United Nations' is now the accepted term, so that every political structure which is admitted to the United Nations is automatically regarded as a nation. All the same, ladies and gentlemen, I consider that we should be extremely wary about applying the word 'nationalism' to what is going on, for instance, in Africa south of the Sahara. When Mr. Lüthy mentions the existence of an African nationalism—a continent-wide nationalism—and then the existence of separate nationalisms in the Congo, the Cameroons, Ghana, Guinea and so forth, and then also the existence of tribal nationalisms, I begin to ask myself what kind of a concept it is that can fit them all. I do not flatter myself that I can delete the term from the international vocabulary; but I personally would be chary of describing all these as nationalism. I think the concept that fits them all is a different one; we might call it the emancipation movement, we might call it the movement for political autonomy; if you insist on an 'ism we can coin a horrible new one and call it 'independentism'; or what you will. But not nationalism, for as Mr. Lüthy took particular care to point out today, these regions, consisting for the most part of former colonial administrative units, now to become nations or States within their old frontiers, have none of the objective features which we, in the course of European history, have come to associate with nationality. And we must not overlook the fact that the national groups in Europe, within the supra-national or multi-national empires, existed as actual historical units before ever they achieved political autonomy. Whereas in Africa it is usually the other way round—a certain territory achieves political autonomy and is admitted to the United Nations as a State, although it possesses not one objective feature that would justify its being designated as a national group or nation in the traditional sense.

A. K. BROHI: . . . *ideals are the masculine principle of history* . . .

I think the greatest historian of Europe, Mr. Fisher, in his introduction to the history of Europe, said that nationalism realizes the post-Protestant phenomenon in Europe. It was after the revolt against the ecclesiastical authority of the Pope in Rome— revolt that was established in the name of the principalities and feudal aristocracies that prevailed in Europe—that nationalism manifested itself. It just came to be as an event in history. There was not a conscious participation in history in terms of some ideas having triumphed. History can be divided into two chapters: the first in which human conduct—whether in its individualized or in its collective aspect—is sanctioned by religion; that is an external sanction. The post-Protestant phenomenon in Europe inaugurates a new chapter in human history in that the locus of the sanctioning power is not outside the individual but is within him. It is really thereafter that human history, in any fundamental sense, is made. Before then there was no history. Human history, in so far as it is responsible, conscious, in so far as the human individual participates and makes history is a post-Protestant phenomenon and fundamentally your European civilization is Protestant in that sense. To the extent to which that consciousness becomes alert, to the extent to which the mind becomes rational and is able to deal with enormous irrational forces which are still operating in history, and constitute its feminine principle, to that extent conscious participation makes it appear that the ideals of enlightened men have found an incarnation and an embodiment in human history.

When we speak about Asian nationalism and African nationalism, the problem seems to me to be simple. Much of that nationalism was inspired by the expansion of the liberal ideals of the West. Most of the pioneers of national movements in the national democracies of Asia and Africa were men educated in the cradle of European civilization. And, consequently, the national movements are imitative in Asia. But that is not the whole story: although they began that way, they are coming into their own. There is a triumphant ascendancy of those ideals. They become more and more associated with material realizations. I think that ideals are the masculine principle of history, but mere masculinity is not creative; it has to have a feminine complement and that feminine complement is furnished by the irrational forces, by the passive, material setting of history. Once man assumes the responsibility of his capacity to fertilize the currents of history, once he sees that the creative process depends on himself, he becomes a responsible historical agent and is participating in history.

PIETER GEYL: . . . *a natural reaction to the denial of fundamental rights* . . .

Mr. Lüthy's paper looks like a diatribe against nationalism. And yet towards the end, he says that he does in the least question the strength or justification of specifically national phenomena or of those rooted in national traditions. He seems quite sympathetic to the demand for autonomy by cultural, religious or even simply regional units for individual freedom of thought or behaviour, permitting individuals as well as historical and social groups to breathe and develop freely, but he adds that such a demand is not in essence nationalistic. Maybe. The word has crude, unpleasant associations and I have myself grown

weary of using it in a positive sense as I used to do in all innocence during a large part of my life. In all innocence, for not only
don't I hold now, but I never held any of these objectionable
opinions which Mr. Lüthy associates with nationalism. I have
never been sufficiently naïve to have believed that a nation arose
from the instinctive action of a native soul—I don't even know
what a native soul is—I care very little for rights and institutions
for the training of national feelings, I detest anything in the
nature of a terrorist ideology that imposes conformity of
thought and behaviour—in fact I regard such conformity as
quite undesirable—and I don't think that it ought to go with the
conception of nationality. As for enmity, suspicion or prejudice
towards other national groups, I am not in the least inclined to
foster any of these feelings. I may say that, even during the occupation of Holland, when I was interned by the occupying authorities for three and a half years, I never allowed myself to
become anti-German. I held fast to the distinction between
National Socialism and the German people. If I may continue to
speak personally, I do not regard the Dutch nation as the salt of
the earth, or the Dutch language as the most beautiful in the
world. I do not shun contact with other national ways of
thinking; I do not want to isolate Holland behind a Chinese wall
of self-complacency. Nevertheless, I feel that a Dutchman
should not try to get rid of his 'Dutchness'. We must remain
Dutch in order to be Europeans.

Now, judging by the passage I quoted in which he admitted
the right of regional communities to breathe and develop freely,
Mr. Lüthy must feel some sympathy with this attitude of mind.
But let me point out that this fundamental right is very often
disregarded by the larger groups or states in which a small
cultural or linguistic community has by the accidental course of
history, become incorporated. Nothing is more inevitable, and
justified, than that such a community should not tamely submit
to the denial of its freedom to breathe and develop. It seems to
me unrealistic to demand of it that it should appeal only to
general human rights when it feels that its own collective rights
are at stake. (And often enough, it will find nothing but indifference on the part of other and more powerful groups.) I submit to
Mr. Lüthy, then, that in the struggle for its rights, nationalism,
that he has held up to scorn, very often signs its origin; its appearance may still be unpleasant but it is well to remember neverthe-

less that in many cases it is the natural response to the denial of fundamental rights. I am confining myself, as you will notice, to an examination of the problem of nationalism of oppressed or at least somewhat unequally treated national groups.

In my youth as a member of the Flemish nationalist movement I had to wage a war on two fronts, against the indifference of Dutch public opinion, on one hand, and against the extremists that shoved themselves within the movement, on the other hand. 'Death to Belgians', Flanders to be joined with Holland in one great Netherland state, demands which flew in the face of history and practical politics. Then when in 1933 National Socialism came into power in Germany, many of the war-impatient and unbalanced Flemish nationalists fell under that pernicious influence. Before the war broke out, I had become isolated, I learned the hard lesson that nationalism, however natural and needful it may be, has a tendency towards extremism. I saw the same thing in Ireland, I saw it in South Africa. There were men among the Flemish nationalists who knew where to stop, but many of them did not. So I learned the hard lesson. Do I now draw the conclusion that the nationalist movement was a mistake from the beginning? And that I ought never to have meddled with it? Certainly not. In the end, a minority of the Flemish nationalists collaborated with the Germans, the nationalists themselves were only a fraction of the Flemish movement, and what the misguided extremists, intoxicated by the slogans of nationalism and absolutism, destroyed, was not Belgium or the peace of the world, they destroyed themselves and the nationalist party. But in the twenties, this party had made a powerful contribution to the regeneration of the Flemish people, to the breaking of the ascendancy of the denationalized upper classes in Flanders, to paving the way for a closer and a culturally fruitful contact between Flanders and Holland, and I remember my close association with it gratefully, and I may say not without some pride.

HUGH SETON-WATSON: . . *the Soviet way of dealing with the national question . . .*

Two distinctions emerge from what we have heard. One is between nationalism as an historical force in Europe, and nationalism as a growing contemporary force in Asia and Africa, and the second is between a movement for national independence and on the other hand, nationalism as an intolerant doctrine in power, using the means of power to oppress other people. It seems very striking that the nationalist movement which came into free expression for a few days in Hungary and —somewhat less openly—for several months in Poland, was an astonishing kind of reversion to the liberal nationalism of the middle of the nineteenth century. I mean the events in Hungary in 1956 were almost a fantastic repetition of 1848: we had the same combination of a desire for liberty, with the willingness to respect other people's liberty and indeed I think probably, a greater willingness on the part of the Hungarian revolution of 1956 to respect the liberty of others than was shown by the Hungarian revolutionaries of Kossuth in 1848, who did not show much respect when they came to the point of the liberties of Croats, Slovaks or other nations. The Hungarian revolution has been retrospectively damned by the Soviets as a Fascist movement and the endless repetition of this calumnious slogan eventually had a certain effect on the minds of West European liberals and socialists who ought to have known better. This is a regrettable fact, but it should not make us blind to the truth, which was that this was a kind of liberal, libertarian nationalism returning to the best traditions. And now, we may look at the Afro-Asians. The problem is very different, I think. The point which I would like to stress is that the peoples of Asia and Africa, and particularly the more recent nationalists of tropical Africa, are bound to come up against all the problems that nationalists came up against in Europe. They don't seem to realize it sufficiently, and this is a thing which somewhat alarms me. I have lately studied Soviet literature on Africa, particularly the *Soviet Journal of Ethnography* and certain oriental studies which devote an enormous amount of attention to the problems of linguistic nationalism and of multi-national states.

The Soviets have built up a very complicated and rather interesting theory, based to some extent on the history of the old Russian Empire and of the Soviet Union, on the evolution of tribes into national groups, national groups into nationalities and nationalities into nations. The theory is very clear, if one studied the subject: their aims are to use the multi-lingual and multi-national characters of the African states to create division and to play them off against each other and eventually impose on all a uniform pattern of Soviet nationality policy. Now the Soviets have their own ready-made formula for dealing with the national question and their aim is to encourage a development in Africa, and in Asia too, of units of a type which they have experienced and manipulated. You impose a totalitarian régime, you encourage a free development for the expression of correct orthodox opinions in all the languages that are spoken; you then proclaim that, unlike in the past, this society is now based on a complete brotherhood of all nations in the state who are no longer oppressing each other, but are brothers, all equal before the law. You proclaim this with a vast propaganda machine. At the same time, you keep the masses of the people mobilized in constant demonstrations and public proclamations of this brotherhood, until the combination of mass propaganda, use of the native language and the whole totalitarian set-up does in fact deal with the problem. Now, it really is striking, considering that the Moslem peoples of the Soviet Union are surrounded by independent Turkey, Persia, Pakistan, Afghanistan and are not so far from India, in all of which countries nationalism is a strong force, that the people of Soviet central Asia have been kept in fact immune to any influence from the other countries.

One might, I think, argue that France could solve the Algerian problem in this manner, using this combination of mobilization, propaganda and preaching of a synthetic doctrine of brotherhood and totalitarian set-up, but on one condition, of course, that is, that the whole people of France became totalitarian, too. And this is a price which the French people will, I think, never pay and God forbid that they should! I am just saying this to show that this sort of thing could be done elsewhere and I suppose if the French Communist party were allowed by Moscow to control Algeria as a matter of tactical convenience, it would in fact try it.

My last point is that the problem of the multi-national state, the problem of linguistic division and the domination of one language group over another language group, is a problem with which we are going to have to live for a very long time. There is no ready-made solution of any kind and our friends in Asia and Africa are going to have to deal with this problem. I have only sympathy for them in their efforts to find a solution, but please let us get away from any kind of idea that the experience of

Europe or the experience of Asia is unique or that there is anything special about the African personality which makes it immune to these difficulties. It seems to me that the doctrine of racialism, of racial superiority or inferiority is odious and utterly unacceptable in any form, including its inverted form, and just as it is utterly insufferable that the White South Africans should say that the Bantus, because they are Bantus, are inferior, so I think it is utterly insufferable that the Africans should think that, because they are Africans, they are immune to these problems of linguistic division themselves or that imperialism is something of which only white people are capable.

JEANNE HERSCH: . . . *nationalism has lost its substantial reality* . . .

I do not agree with Mr. Brohi, that real history begins with the Reformation. I quite agree that from the standpoint from which he approaches the matter, the Reformation constitutes a decisive turning-point. But I do not think we can say that it represents the beginning of conscious history, because then we should have to concede that conscious history began with a radical distinction, a struggle, between the two—the masculine and the feminine—principles involved. Whereas I believe that there was a kind of affectionate thought, of thinking affection— that there was a thoughtful way of loving, a loving way of thinking; and I do not believe we can date the inception of history from the more radical disruption of those links.

The real human revolutions are undertaken on behalf of beloved things, or beings, with the intention of enabling them to exist. In other words, change is effected out of love for something which exists—under inappropriate circumstances, but which does exist.

And now, what about nationalism? I think nationalism has changed its sex. At certain periods of past history, nationalism had a weighty feminine aspect. At certain other periods—though this is a mere outline and I cannot go into much detail—it was probably, so to speak, a couple, with a dual life. And nowadays nationalism, even when it arises in the countries that are seeking independence for the first time, is a male principle, in the meaning we have attributed to it; in other words, it is an ideology; in fact it is a pass-word, a sign—a banner, if you like. It has divested itself of its former material substance. And I think that nationalism can no longer, as Mr. Polanyi's paper hints, act as a revival of substance and weight on the political and ideological horizon of the present day.

In this respect I entirely agree with Mr. Lüthy; we have to invent something else. But that brings us up against the paradox inherent in our situation—a paradox that dooms our discussions, however intelligent and interesting they may be, to a sterility not confined to our meeting here, but extending to the whole present-day effort to think things out. For the fact is that we are trying to arrive by way of thought—by an effort of subtle, detached thought—at a weight of attachment which cannot be reached, invented, suggested by thought. It is almost as though we were trying to create something ancient, to conceive of something substantial and give substance to our conception. And that, in my opinion, is the essential difficulty that confronts us today in our search for what we feel we lack and must have. Mr. Lüthy suggested that federalism might be the path to take. In my opinion it is the only proper path on the level on which the problem of nationalism arises; but that proper path, the path of federalism, must be correctly understood, so as never to lose sight of the element of weight and of established, longstanding fact that must be included in it.

CZESLAW MILOSZ: . . . *the content depends on the social structure . . .*

I am a Pole and every Pole is a rabid nationalist and is lacking in international feeling, so I am in a happy position here that, not being a scholar who looks at national problems from a detached attitude, I can jump with both my feet into the pie. If I understand Mr. Lüthy well, he would like to purify the struggle for independence in Africa and Asia from the stain of nationalism or of nationalist doctrines as they were elaborated in Europe. In any case, this is a question of terminology, because in Continental Europe we use the term 'nationalism' to designate a certain national doctrine while, in the Anglo-Saxon world, it has a different meaning. I agree completely with Mr. Lüthy that in Europe we never use the term 'nationalism' because it has very unpleasant connotations. Progressive movements of the beginning of the nineteenth century became more and more reactionary and bloodthirsty up to recent times and we witnessed many terrible things during the last war. Yet even in the national doctrine immediately preceding the last war, we should make certain distinctions. It depended very much upon the structure of a given society. In such purely peasant societies as the Baltic States or the Ukraine, nationalism had a clear class character, it was a peasant nationalism and, curiously enough, it was connected with a movement of creating co-operatives, not co-operatives in the *kolkhoz* sense, but organizations for the marketing of agricultural products. One basic and important factor has not been mentioned here, connected with what is called today mass culture. We have been witnessing during our lifetime a progressive russification of Russia: I mean that a Russian who before the Revolution had a very small share in the Russian national heritage, became, through millions of editions of so-called Russian classics, much more Russian than he was before the Revolution. This phenomenon repeats itself everywhere and is very clearly visible in the eastern part of Europe with the consequence that Poles become more Polish, Hungarians more Hungarian, Russians more Russian. From this point of view, I find that a study of the time of Pushkin, at the beginning of the nineteenth century, can teach us much more about the present development in Russia than the study of Marx. This factor introduces enormous changes and we witness a breakdown of nationalist doctrines as they were elaborated before the last war. For instance, in such countries as Poland or Hungary, the whole nationalist doctrine was completely broken down and suppressed, in my opinion with rather happy results. So it is no wonder that national feelings visible in the Hungarian Revolution bore some features of the big uprising of '48, because the national reactionary doctrine broke down in such countries as Hungary or Poland, while national feeling has taken other, more attractive forms. Thus I would reproach one thing to Mr. Lüthy: his detached attitude, his lack of sympathy for nationalism, are by no means his peculiar characteristics and they were shared by many progressive minds in Eastern Europe. They fought against nationalistic doctrines but the result was that they were throwing away the baby together with the bath-water.

The tragedy of many Polish progressive movements was that they abandoned the monopoly of national feeling to the most reactionary and right-wing circles, the error for instance of Rosa

Luxemburg, who did not take into account the particular national factors, was one of the reasons for the total defeat of the Polish Communist Party. It is a general tendency of international Socialism and Communism to neglect what is particular of a certain situation in a given country and it explains their falling completely under the rule of the Kremlin.

EHSAN NARAGHI: *. . . traditional roots . . .*

Nationalism had been referred to as a calamity; certain forms of it have been extolled, others have been deplored. I think this is a rather abstract approach to the problem. At any rate, as far as the Middle East and my own country—Iran—are concerned, I can safely say that nationalism has frequently been a movement grouping and assembling the most various elements, and that it has represented both a tribute to the feeling of justice, of lawful, democratic government and a tribute to the ideals of the past. I therefore disagree with my friend Professor Hourani when he says that Middle Eastern nationalism is too rationalistic and nihilistic.

I would say that if Middle Eastern nationalism had not been rooted in tradition and impelled by religious force, it could never have succeeded as a movement. Take Iran as an example, even though it is true that conditions were different there from those in other Arab countries, because Iran had never been occupied by a foreign colonial power. In 1906, when the first democratic movements for the establishment of a lawful, democratic government were launched, there was a surge of anti-foreign feeling as a reaction against Russian pressure; but at the same time there was considerable religious support; it was the priests, the *mullahs,* who were in the forefront of this movement and who extolled the religious principles of the Koran, accusing the Government of abandoning those principles and of lapsing into nihilism. The subsequent movements, too, were inspired to a great extent by religious feelings. I would say that in the Middle East the prime consideration is the search for lawful government and a feeling of justice, rather than an inspiration towards social and economic development.

This is a point on which our Western friends are often mistaken. The Middle East does not begin by calculations, those countries do not look at problems in the same way as the West does: questions of national income, investment and so forth are often the calculations of experts, which do not reflect the feelings of those whose foremost aspiration is to arrive at a measure of lawful government.

ALTIERO SPINELLI: *... patriotism and nationalism ...*

I do not know whether nationalism is male or female; but whatever its sex may be it undoubtedly manages to have a great many husbands or a great many wives. For if we regard nationalism as a certain feeling of solidarity among the members of a particular group of people—solidarity which is usually based on language and tradition, solidarity which in some cases is felt only by an *élite*, while in other cases it extends to large sections of the population—we find that it may serve as a principle of integration, or that it may play a part in various combinations. In some instances the purpose of nationalism is to promote a certain separatism, to defend the autonomy of a particular group within an established political system; this is the case with the Flemish national movement. Then there is another nationalism, which is prompted by the definite wish to become independent of a foreign power, as for instance, Italian nationalism. German nationalism, on the other hand, was not directed against any foreign power. Nationalism of former colonial peoples is a search for freedom and so are nationalist forces within the Soviet Empire. There is also a nationalism which is the factor of human solidarity resulting directly from the dangers of wartime, summoned up by the appeals to tradition, by exhortations to defend home, parents, etc. This form of nationalism is to be met with everywhere where there is a war going on—even under régimes which are not and do not wish to be nationalistic; Russian leaders, for instance, appealed during the war to national feeling, though with some degree of cold political calculation, that is to say with the desire to make use of a certain form of integration additional to that which was really the *raison d'être* of the system itself.

In all these cases, defence of a cultural system, desire for independence, defence against military aggression, nationalism—or one might say patriotism—has its attractive aspects. It also has less attractive aspects, for it frequently incites people to hate their fellow-men simply because they speak a different language and have different traditions; but I would say that in any event it is never unduly dangerous. In cases where it is directed against established authority it even has a certain absolute value, because it is always a good thing for the established authority to encounter a certain resistance.

But we have been led, in our own day, to speak of nationalism as a poison, an illness, because nationalism can form yet another affinity; it may become the principle that upholds authority, it may ally itself to the established authority; and I think the word 'nationalism' should be reserved for such cases as this, the term 'patriotism' being used for the others. Nationalism in this sense was born not very long ago; I would even say that it was invented by the French during the French Revolution, when they abolished the legitimacy of royalty. During the French Revolution the Girondins tried to establish the principle of a community based on freedom; but this experiment soon collapsed —whereas it had proved successful in America a few years earlier. The nation was set up in place of the king. The nation was the legitimate embodiment of authority. The French Revolution gave rise to two parallel types of legitimate authority, national and democratic—the will of the people and the will of the nation. And that has survived until the present day, when we see that the man who wields the power in France, de Gaulle, believes that the French people are merely confirming a legitimate authority which is not constituted by the French people but by France—by the nation.

After the French had invented this principle—almost involuntarily, because in its early days the French Revolution wanted to be cosmopolitan—it was applied in other European countries and developed into a malady that spread all over the continent. I think Lüthy was correct in saying that during the nineteenth and twentieth centuries it acted as the principle of organization, of integration, in the system of European communities. This does not mean that it found universal application; but we find in history that whenever a movement succeeded in invoking the national principle as its justification for starting a war, for destroying one State or creating another, there was always a prejudice in its favour. And that favourable prejudice continued right up to the end of the attempt to unite all Germans in the Third Reich. Even when Hitler wanted to seize Austria, the Sudetenland and so forth, the rest used to say 'After all, what he wants is quite fair'—in accordance with the principle that all the members of a nation must belong to one State and that the *raison d'être* of a State is the nation.

Now when a State is based on the nation it has an inevitable tendency towards totalitarianism—towards a situation in which the individual citizen becomes a mere tool which has to obey the established authority because that authority is serving the nation—that new idea, one might almost say that new divinity. The experience that Europe has undergone, was and still is—for we have not yet emerged from it—a fundamentally negative experience. This experience should compel us to meditate over our history in order to show what were the fatal elements first in the Italian and German movements, and then in the First World War, which checked the attempt to endow Europe with a supra-national organization. It was an attempt which began in 1815 in Vienna and which might have had further developments. We Europeans should feel a certain obligation to warn the new States which are now being formed in Africa and Asia against this danger, by constantly reminding them that it is one thing to have a community with certain characteristics and traditions which this community wishes to defend and is entitled to defend —a community on the principle of placing the authority at the service of the citizens, since this is the foundation of freedom; and that it is quite a different thing—though the tendency easily arises, because patriotic feelings exist everywhere—to seek for the principle of integration along the easier road by saying 'Let us try to form a nation'. There may always be a tendency to consider that it doesn't matter very much if the nation does not exist at the outset—if there are only separate tribes with different traditions. The most firmly-established nation in the world to-day is the French nation; and it is one which was created by the central authority. In the case of the Italians, the nation may be said to have existed before the State; but that cannot be said of France, for France was created by the French State. In a continent like Africa, where every possibility still lies open, new paths may be chosen, but there is also the risk that undesirable examples may be followed, in ignorance of the dangers. It would be very dangerous if the idea were to gain ground that nationalism, of no matter what kind—that of Senegal, that of the Congo, that of Africa as a whole—should be the foundation of the State. That is a negative principle and should be rejected.

128

Criticism and Discussion

FRANÇOIS BONDY: .. *the impracticable German national-ism* ...

I feel that here in Berlin it is not possible to talk about nationalism in general, without saying a few words about the very special and very central problem of 'German nationalism'. For when I heard Professor Hofer say just now that there had been certain instances of successful national integration during the nineteenth century, I was reminded that yesterday, at a very stirring meeting held on that very stirring date—June 17th—the Prime Minister of a German 'Land' said that the relations between Germany and Poland should be based on the fact that certain frontiers had been established by treaties in the fourteenth and fifteenth centuries. The Poles among us were extremely surprised, and there were others, too, who felt no inclination to support this German claim, because so much has happened since the fifteenth century, and particularly in our own century. When we think of the twentieth century and of the nineteenth, we have to recognize that there have been many instances of the successful integration of a people into a State and nation. By and large it was, I think, successful in France; it succeeded in the Scandinavian countries—partly through integration and partly through disintegration; it went without saying in the British Isles, and to a certain extent the Irish have brought it off too. The same applies to Italy, Spain and Portugal. But there is one country in Europe—in the centre of Europe, its greatest continental power, Germany—where integration has, in my opinion, never succeeded and never can succeed. When one reflects on the fact that nationalism is insufficient for Europe as a formative and liberating principle, it seems to me that Germany inevitably comes to mind. In 1848 the democratic idea of German unification was shared by all German-speaking peoples; the Alsatians approved of it, the German-speaking Austrians approved of it, and in France the Left, the democrats, went much further than Bismarck. Marx and Engels were ready to launch a campaign against all Germany's neighbours and to see the Czech language abolished, for the sake of this historical unity of the German language. But nothing came of it. When the German national idea is identified with the German language it has to take an imperialistic form. As certain historians, such as Golo Mann and Ludwig Dehio, have

129

shown, there are always two alternative demands: either for a German Reich established according to the historical frontiers, which means including peoples that are not German-speaking; or for a German Reich based on the German language, which means including peoples which have no desire to belong to the German Federation—such as the Swiss, the Alsatians and so forth. So it seems to me that Germany, in the centre of Europe, constitutes a sort of camp set up among the other nations, which makes the national principle impossible. And precisely because yesterday, June 17th, we were reminded of the aspiration towards the reunification of the free and the oppressed Germans and of the German workers' uprising—with which all of us here, of course, are in deepest sympathy—I think it is a good thing to reflect that our feeling of solidarity arose out of the fact that on that occasion there were no nationalist songs and no discordantly nationalistic note was struck; there was undoubtedly a national aspiration to reunify the historic Germany that is now divided, but certain demands of a social, cultural and humanistic nature were very much to the fore. And since in the course of history German nationalism has been less concerned with the claims of humanism than other forms of nationalism, it has a greater need than other forms of nationalism to be elevated by other principles, which we might call federative ones. It is no mere accident that 'The Marseillaise', although it is such a bloodthirsty song, sends a thrill of brotherly feeling through men in all the five continents, for it has a kind of universal, liberating attraction. Whereas as we found yesterday, the German national song, composed by Hoffmann von Fallersleben, beautiful and noble though it is, awakens no response in non-Germans. German nationalism, as such, embodies a principle which is narrow, yet carries a certain risk of explosion; and we, who look forward to liberation and freedom for all Germans and all other East Europeans, should stipulate that here, in particular, this idea of liberation must be kept most carefully free from any discordant nationalistic note.

THEODOR LITT: . . . *the European duty of the Germans* . . .

I think the hearts of all the Germans in this assembly were touched, for Mr. Bondy laid his finger on the whole tragedy of Germany's destiny and on Germany's well-known errors too. I think that in reply I can say: When we consider historical circumstances we should be careful not to assume that a solution exists for every given situation. People are always going up to heads of States and to those responsible for deciding spiritual matters, and demanding that they find a solution for some complicated situation in which they are involved. I think we shall never have a clear grasp of history unless we realize that certain situations are insoluble and that the only way of dealing with them is to overstep the boundaries of what have hitherto been the accepted forms of life. The terrible fate we are suffering is due to the failure of the German nation to make its national frontiers and its political limits coincide. And I agree that we Germans must desist from basing our claim to frontiers to which we believe we have title, on historical memories. On the contrary we should open our eyes to the fact that what has happened in East Germany has led to such a confusion of territorial boundaries and cultural commitments, that it is impossible to conceive of any historical solution that might bring them to a completely satisfactory conclusion. We have to remember that the first man to present the national idea to us Germans was Johann Gottfried Herder. When we read what he wrote about the wealth of the nations and the fullness of the divine life that manifests itself in the course of historical existence, we see at once that nothing was further from his mind than to put forward, on behalf of the nation, any kind of claim to political frontiers.

It is bad enough that in the course of its development, and especially within the last forty years, the German nation should have strayed so far from this free and open interpretation of nationality. We have indeed paid dearly for that. But one thing seems clear to me; that in a world that is struggling to find its form, we Germans cannot expect to find a satisfactory place for ourselves anywhere, unless we make a determined return to the greatness, the richness and freedom of Herder's interpretation of the nation. That interpretation, it seems to me, would also show us that we can find a satisfactory existence only in a world and in a Europe where the frontiers of individual States have become a secondary consideration. So long as State frontiers are regarded as setting up a division between the people who live on either side of them, there can be no satisfactory coexistence between different nations. And this leads me to the opinion that if we are now to struggle for the concept of

Europe and the form Europe is to take in future, we Germans, by reason of our terrible sufferings in the course of history, should come forward as the chief representatives of the pure, ideal concept of Europe; for it represents our only prospect of achieving a satisfactory existence from the political standpoint as well. And if this meeting has helped the German participants to become more aware of this historical mission, it will have been no small practical achievement.

FRODE JAKOBSEN: . . . *in Asia, a feeling of responsibility* . . .

I had an experience in the Philippines a year ago which was something very enlightening for me, as a European visiting Asia for the first time. It brought home to me our frequent habit of calling quite different things by the same name, which is a source of misunderstanding. Professor Lüthy said that not all the efforts to achieve independence can be described as nationalism in our sense of the word. I would go a bit further, for my experience was that suddenly, in conversation with people who called themselves Philippine nationalists, I realized that the term nationalism meant something quite different for them from what I had supposed. I had come to these people in a sceptical mood, because I am well acquainted with European nationalism. But if you ask me to explain what nationalism meant for them, I would say that it meant having a sense of responsibility not only for one's own family—which may be customary in Asia—or for a group of some kind, but for the whole nation. Their nationalism was in no way opposed to internationalism, competition with other nations played no part in it; it even had nothing to do with the fight for independence. They called themselves nationalists, and their nationalism consisted in that they— enlightened and prosperous townspeople—used to go out to poverty-stricken villages to show the village women how to nourish their children better, and thus reduce the high infantile mortality rate; to show the peasants how to build houses that are healthier to live in, and how to plant rice so as to get the best yield from it. Thus there are people we call nationalists, and who call themselves nationalists, who define nationalism as a feeling of responsibility not only for oneself, for one's own family, but for the larger unit known as the nation. This kind of nationalism builds up a nation from within and need not, as we are apt to assume, have anything to do with foreign countries. I saw that very clearly in the Philippines. But I think I came across the same thing in other parts of Asia as well. Nationalism in the bad sense is to be found in Asia too, of course—I have no illusions as to that. But I feel that we in the West should pay more heed to this particular element in what is known as nationalism.

RICHARD LOWENTHAL: . . . *the nation is formed by democratic participation* . . .

I am one of those who consider that the feeling or consciousness of nationality plays a more positive role than Mr. Lüthy believes. But I think his paper did great service by calling attention to the dangerous vagueness of the concept of nationality as a criterion for the creation of a State. If one rejects—as Mr. Lüthy does, as I do, and as I believe all of us in this assembly do—the nationalistic view of the metaphysics of history; if we refuse to believe that the various nations are directly God-given, that they existed from the beginning of history although they only gradually awoke to the realization that their common blood or common speech had set each of them apart, once and for all: if we reject all this, then the question that naturally arises, as it has now arisen so acutely in connection with Africa, for example, is the question of how one defines a nation, or how a nation defines itself. And it seems to me that we have not yet produced a completely satisfactory answer to that question, except Professor Geyl in one of his comments. The point is that a nation is not something that has existed from the very first: a nation is brought into being by certain typical historical events, by those events which determine in what form, at what stage and within what boundaries a community awakens to a realization that its members are participants in all its concerns. In other words, a nation's first awareness of itself as such, and its awareness of democracy are closely-related historical developments. Professor Geyl himself belongs to a nation that offers a very admirable example of this. If we try to define the Dutch from the point of view of language, we find that they originally spoke a form of Low German. The Dutch nation came to definite form through the fact that in the battle against the Spanish domination, this northern part of Holland, and only this part, succeeded in winning its freedom and established democratic institutions for itself. We can see very similar things happening in our own day. There has been some mention of the German linguistic frontiers in this meeting. Let us consider the extremely interesting case of the German-speaking Austrians. Around and after 1848, after the constitution of Bismarck's Reich, and even after 1918, a great proportion of the Germans in Austria, who subsequently lived in the new Austrian State, felt themselves to be Germans and regarded their State as a temporary structure, created solely as a result of the ban on union with Germany which was laid down in the Treaty of Versailles. After this feeling of German nationality on the part of the Austrians had been defeated on various occasions—in 1848, in 1860–71 and in 1918 —their wish was given a semblance of fulfilment by Hitler's annexation of Austria. The result was that under the impression of this experience the Germans of Austria lost their feeling of being Germans and now really feel themselves to be Austrians— members of the Austrian nation—as treaties had earlier declared them to be, but without their being truly so. In this sense I believe that the question of what a nation is, does not permit of any hard and fast reply; the reply emerges in the course of historical development, and in many countries has done so only in our own time. There is no reason, *a priori*, why the boundaries of such nations should be fixed in the light of linguistic unity. There is in fact no *a priori* criterion to determine where their frontiers should lie. It depends much more upon the circumstances in which they attained independence, upon the development of their new States. Any group that can combine to set up a viable State in which all sections of the population can play a part, will develop into a nation. And I think it is important for us to recognize that there should be no attempt to anticipate that development by applying any particular theory on the subject. Now if this is so it becomes clear, it seems to me, that there is a great gulf between this concept of the nation as resulting from a process of democratic participation, and any kind of metaphysical concept; and also that the democratic concept of what constitutes a nation does not provide any ground for setting up the nation as the highest value—any justification for nationalism in the German sense of the term.

In conclusion I would like to say something about the view that federalism and nationalism are contrasting terms. I think it is no accident that Mr. Lüthy is Swiss. Historically speaking Switzerland is unique, because its democratic institutions were set up at a time when nationalism had not developed, and in federal form. I do not think it would be possible in the world of today, to substitute federal institutions in place of the institutions of national self-determination. The only possibility is to set them up as supra-national institutions of self-determination. A form of federalism that declared itself to be a nihilistic negation of the national concept, would be inconsistent unless it denied democracy as well. In this sense, Metternich was the only consistent anti-nationalist who ever existed.

SIDNEY HOOK: . . *institutions permitting differences of quality* . . .

The substance of this discussion confirms a principle first announced by Aristotle and restated by a great jurist, Justice Holmes, who said that general principles by themselves never decide specific or individual cases. We grant that nationalism is a general expression of the right to self-determination and that even in some of its problematic forms it cannot be excommunicated. Nationalism is something like a children's disease, it has to be gone through to be transcended, and like children's diseases, the later in time a group acquires nationalism, the more violent its form, especially if its aspirations have been repressed.

As a rationalist, I quite agree with Professor Litt that some problems may be insoluble, but I am not prepared to resign myself to the recognition of the problem as insoluble until we apply as much creative intelligence as possible to its resolution. I thought that Professor Jakobsen, whose experiences in the Philippines I shared, would call our attention to some aspect of this difficulty, because when I was young and naïve, I always assumed that Scandinavian countries would illustrate the road by which nationalism could be transcended, but I think there are certain events, even in the history of Scandinavian countries, which show how difficult it is to develop a unified culture which would be accepted as expressing the legitimate interests of national groups.

I agree with Mr. Lowenthal when he says that you can't substitute the concept of federalism for that of nationalism. But I wonder whether we shouldn't use our creative, rational powers to find a new conception of federalism. So far as our deliberations have been descriptive, we have been weak in presenting plans for possible action and organization. Nobody has spoken about nationalism in America and the United States, but it presents an interesting illustration of how a culture can be developed from the most plural and diverse origins; the thirteen American colonies were profoundly different in religion, to some extent even in language, and with the immigration to the United States, the great problem was to forge a nation. Now that nation was forged with a conception that what was to unite people would be a certain type of institution that would permit any quality of difference so that no group would feel that what was legitimate to them in terms of cultural values would be overridden. Now there is some danger in that too, a conception of a melting-pot in which all cultures would be dipped and then they would emerge in some kind of shining quality undistinguishable from each other. But that is a difficulty that can be met in terms of indigenous procedures; but particularly for Europe, Asia and Africa, what I think we should now turn our attention to, is a conception of a common administrative unit which does not impose upon the sense of uniqueness that each national group feels.

ALBERT HOURANI: . . . *there cannot be a philosophy of the nation . . .*

I should like to correct a misunderstanding of my position which Mr. Naraghi put forward when he interpreted me as saying that certain aspects of Asian and specifically of Middle Eastern nationalism were rationalistic. My thought was rather the opposite and I think everything that has been said rather confirms it. I am more and more convinced that one can say nothing about nationalism in itself, because it is not a concept. Essentially, nationalism is a feeling of solidarity and natural attraction which binds certain people together. Other people's nationalism is as incomprehensible, and even as absurd as other people's love.

But the moral neutrality of nationalism is precisely its moral danger. The differences between nationalisms of today and the sentimental tribal solidarity of the past is that, for various social and technical necessities, today we have to encourage nationalism, to formulate it articulately, to instil it in people's minds. We do this by putting it in words, that is to say by grafting on to it certain concepts which have essentially nothing to do with it, and this nationalism is not itself a concept allowing a systematic development, since there cannot strictly be a philosophy of the nation. It lies open equally to all ideals, whether ideals of the rights of man, ideals of religion and so on. It might be thought that this, as Professor Hook said, is only a passing phase, that once nations have achieved their independence, they will recover from the child's disease of nationalism and will be able to think about something else. I don't myself believe that this is so, because I think that there still are, in the present world, for independent national States, problems for which it is necessary and natural to try to generate a feeling of national unity and loyalty.

HERBERT LÜTHY: ... *nationalistic falsification of history* ...

The chief result of this discussion has been to show that nationalism cannot be defined, but that it can very well be mobilized and very easily be put to ill use, precisely because it cannot be defined. This was expressed in the papers—including, as I was reminded, my own—because of course everyone speaks in the light of his own background, his own experience, his own world. Before this discussion someone told me that in my paper the Swiss schoolmaster disappeared. I don't deny it, I quite agree; and it is doubly true. For one thing the schoolmaster, or rather the historian has done so, because to me a century of nationalistic writing of history to serve the purpose of national integration—a century of nationalistic writing of history, falsification of history, blurring of history—constitutes something so horrible that it often makes me feel guilty about my profession. Secondly, schoolmasters have been one of the chief instruments of nationalism in Europe, and Swiss schoolmasters, of course, because it is true that we are a State that arose in a pre-nationalistic period, and in which what Madame Jeanne Hersch has defined as the female type of nationalism, which I would call simply a feeling of directly belonging to a small community in one's own land, to the community one knows and works with, the original, genuine community feeling—has survived the nationalistic epoch. We live on an island, which has probably intensified our awareness of the extent to which the wide-scale nationalism of the nineteenth century (I repeat, wide-scale not by present-day standards, but by those of the period) was an artificial ideology—fabricated, of course, in the interests of power-politics. From which it also follows that if we, in this assembly, reject nationalism as a doctrine, as a principle of integration, that does not signify rejection of the right to existence of separate communities, but the recognition of that right for all of them. That is the meaning of federalism. And though Professor Geyl thought he was contradicting me, I was almost tempted to embrace him, because what he calls nationalism— the right to existence of the Flemish language and the Flemish people—is what I would call separatism or autonomism, the preliminary requisite for which is, precisely, a federative, pluralistic organization for coexistence—which of course confirms the destiny of Flemish nationalism as nationalism, but also gives an example of the innumerable possibilities for the abuse of such a movement, its use as a fifth column in international affairs.

WALTHER HOFER: . . . *European colonialism and Soviet imperialism* . . .

We have spoken, in relation to nationalism, of the East European situation, of the situation in Asia and of the situation in Africa. I would like to take the opportunity of this meeting, in which so many distinguished men and women from all over the world are participating, to call attention to a circumstance that is quite obvious, but which has not been mentioned today—the fact that under the same international conditions in which the African and Asian nations have succeeded in gaining their freedom, the Eastern European nations have been compelled to give up their freedom. In the light of psychology and history we can well understand that, as it seems to me, a great number of our friends in Asia and Africa hesitate to recognize a parallel between European colonialism in their continents and Soviet imperialism in Eastern Europe. But I think we should be mistaken if we drew the conclusion from this, that the oppression of the East European nations which have come under the Soviet yoke is not as terrible as that from which the Asian and African peoples were suffering. I also believe that the sympathy shown by the intellectuals in what is known as the Western world has played and is still playing a great, decisive role in supporting the independence movements among the African and Asian peoples. And I would like to appeal to our friends, the Asian and African intellectuals, to do the same in their turn, by encouraging their own countries not to forget those nations which have lost their freedom at the very time when they themselves were winning it.

The Role of Religion in the Pursuit of Freedom

KATHLEEN BLISS

ELIEF has its origins in belonging. We hold the beliefs we
share about man because we belong in the European
tradition. Can we accept articulately this belonging to
the whole of that tradition? To some of our contemporaries the
defeat of religion was the necessary prerequisite of man's intellectual freedom and the rise of science. The clashes that took
place are to them the archetypes of an inevitable hostility. May
it not, however, be the case that belief needs the acids of criticism and science the background of assured beliefs consciously
and responsibly accepted as such (namely as beliefs and not as
substitutes for science in its own sphere)? It is important for
Christians to accept what Bonhoeffer wrote in his book on
Ethics which he drafted in prison here in Berlin between 1943
and 1945, 'Intellectual honesty in all things including questions
of belief was the great achievement of emancipated reason and
it has ever since been one of the indispensable moral require-
ments of western man. Contempt for the age of rationalism is a
suspicious sign of failure to feel the need for truthfulness.'
What, therefore, we need to search for is not a device to help
man to continue to feel responsible or important, but the truth
about him as far as we are ever able, from within the human
situation, to discover it.

There seem to me to be two contributions at this point from
the side of religion. In the first place and negatively, Christianity
asks the question whether the secularized version of the Christian story, which puts man at the centre of man's concern, does
not deprive man of something he needs in order to be man—
an object of worship of which he can use the sublimest words

141

without either lowering the meaning of the words or making a God out of himself.

In the second place, I would suggest that the commonly felt human objection to be nothing more than part of the natural order, nothing more than an extremely complicated and sensitive machine for reacting to our environment in the interests of our survival, has its true explanation in the religious, and supremely in the Christian, understanding of man. In the midst of our life and activity we are visited by grace, that is by powers of which we know we are not the authors. We hear and respond to our calling. 'I can fully discover myself,' writes Gabriel Marcel, 'only in so far as I respond to a call which comes to me from beyond where I now am.' I am not left to *make* life meaningful in the teeth of total meaninglessness, as Sartre would say. 'I find myself as I discover an inner bond with others in shared ideas and shared feelings.'

I have already mentioned Dietrich Bonhoeffer. He was the son of a well-known German doctor and psychiatrist who taught in the University of Berlin. He entered the Lutheran Church as a pastor and after a period of study in America became a theological teacher in Berlin. He became deeply disturbed by the degree to which the churches, like the universities and almost every other institution in Germany, were being dragged along in passive acceptance of Nazi doctrines and practices. After being forbidden to lecture in Berlin by the Nazis, he withdrew to England where, as pastor of a German congregation, he carried on his protest. He was soon recalled to Germany to take charge of an emergency theological college for the training of young ministers for the emerging 'confessing' church which was forming in resistance. Here he wrote books which were widely discussed in Germany and helped to draw a wide circle of Christians into steady resistance to the Nazis. Through his brother-in-law, Bonhoeffer had contacts with the German generals who later plotted an attack on Hitler's life. When war broke out in 1939, he was in the United States and was begged to stay. He decided to return and throw himself into the work of the confessing church. He was forbidden to lecture, preach, write or remain in Berlin. But the confessing church grew in strength. Meanwhile the same stirrings were taking place in the Roman Catholic Church. Helmuth von Moltke was adviser to the German supreme command on international law. As such he used the opportunities which came his way to warn the intended victims of the Nazis in occupied countries, and many Jews owed their survival to him. In 1942 he wrote to a friend in England, 'It is beginning to dawn on a not too numerous, but active, part of the population not that they have been misled, not that they are in for a hard time, not that they might lose the war, but that what is being done is sinful . . . Perhaps you will remember that in discussions before the war I used to maintain that belief in God was not essential for coming to the results you arrive at. Today I know I was wrong, completely wrong. You know that I have fought the Nazis from the first day, but the amount of risk and readiness for sacrifice which is asked from us now require more than right principles, especially as we know that the success of our fight will probably mean a total collapse as a national unit!' Von Moltke was arrested, tried and shot, along with a group of his friends. The chief accusation against them was that they had 'discussed with Jesuit priests and Protestant ministers the possibility of Nazi collapse'. 'This gives us,' he wrote on the eve of his execution, 'the inestimable advantage of being killed for something which (*a*) we really have done and (*b*) is worth while.'

Bonhoeffer spent almost two years in prison in Berlin, from 1943 to 1945, during which time he wrote the outline of a great work on Ethics. He was hanged on April 9th. All his life he spent in the pursuit of freedom, for himself and others. In his *Ethics* he speaks of it as the life of a man who is committed to 'the double bond with others and with God'. 'Without this bond and this freedom there is no responsibility,' he wrote. Among his last papers, written as he was being carried from place to place with other prisoners in front of the advancing armies of the Allies, was a poem. 'Not a good poem', he wrote, 'but I'm no poet. It expresses my ideas.' It is called 'Stations on the Road to Freedom'. It contains what any Christian would want to put into the concept of freedom; the note of overcoming death. Freedom demands first a body disciplined to obey your will, since the secret of freedom is learned only by way of control. Next, action: 'Bravely take hold of the real, not dallying with what might be. Not in the flight of ideas but only in action is freedom': but action is succeeded by suffering; the hands that were active are bound; helpless and alone you see the end of your deed and commit your freedom into the hand of God.

143

Finally, 'O death, cast off the chains and lay low the thick walls of our mortal bodies and blinded souls that at last we may behold what here we failed to see. O Freedom, long have we sought thee in discipline and in action and in suffering. Dying we behold thee now and see thee in the face of God.'

Christian Values and Freedom
JOSEPH PIEPER

IT is an undeniable fact that 'religion' or, to be more precise, the Churches and a number of individuals impelled by strong religious convictions, have made a stand against tyranny, whether in its National Socialist or its Bolshevik form, and have been active in the cause of freedom (and not merely of 'religious' freedom). But I do not believe this indicates that the opposition between out and out secular rationalism and liberalism on the one hand, and religion on the other, is based on a misunderstanding which this experience justifies us in dismissing once and for all. The general programme of our Congress includes a statement that may be summed up as follows: 'During the eighteenth century religion was the arch-enemy of freedom; but it proved to be a stronghold of resistance to tyranny under the Third Reich.' That 'but' conveys astonishment. But I see no reason for astonishment. One could say, with a little exaggeration, that the reason for which religion was the enemy of freedom in the eighteenth century—and remains so, even nowadays, from the point of view of liberal rationalism—was the very same reason that led religion (i.e. the Church and certain strongly religious individuals) to resist government by tyranny. This is an indication of the complexity of the problems we have to tackle when we begin to inquire whether religion is a help or a hindrance to the achievement of freedom.

It is true, of course, that both liberalism and Christianity have fought for freedom. But it must be remembered that they did so for very different reasons and with very different aims. And it is about these differences that I would like to say a few words.

Mrs. Bliss was perfectly justified in quoting Count Helmuth von Moltke in her paper. But I cannot recall any passage in his letters which suggests that that noble man, who was actuated by consciously Christian motives, ever offered resistance in defence of 'the idea of freedom', or that he fought and died in the specific cause of 'freedom'. The same can be said of many others who rose up against tyranny because of their religious convictions. Moreover, the official utterances of the Church make few specific references to freedom. They say much more about truth, about justice and injustice, about human dignity and the disregard shown for it, about parents' right to bring up their children as they think fit—and so forth. They do, of course, call for freedom as well. And of course Christians, like other people, regard freedom as a fundamental, indispensable and indisputable right. No amount of talk will obliterate from the history of Christianity certain shameful and terrible episodes such as the Inquisition; but it must be borne in mind that they were entirely contrary to the theories of Christianity itself. Whereas the crimes of the totalitarian régimes, whether National Socialist or Bolshevik, were the logical consequence of their own principles. (St. Thomas Aquinas, who lived in the time of the Inquisition, went so far as to say that those who thought it wrong to believe in Christ were not allowed to believe in him; and that it was better for a man to die in a state of excommunication than to disobey his own conscience.) But the 'concept of freedom' plays a very different part in Christian doctrine from the one it plays in the rationalistic and liberal view of the world. I do not think any liberal would say there could be such a thing as too much freedom; he might not even admit that freedom could be misused. Whereas Christians are very decidedly of that opinion. There can never be too much justice, of course, and to speak of a misuse of justice would be nonsense. But freedom can very definitely be misused.

There is another difference, and to my mind an even more important one, between Christian and liberal attitudes towards freedom. In order to understand it, we must remember that the 'idea' of freedom is one thing and the 'reality' of freedom is another thing. One characteristic of the Christian view of freedom is, I believe, the conviction that in the history of mankind, there are certain things that can become realities only on condition that they are not specifically regarded and proclaimed as 'ideas'. There are obviously certain things to which we can never attain if we expressly or even exclusively strive for them. They come to us *adventitiously*, when we are expressly aiming at something else. This is a theory that has other applications as well; psychoanalysts have discovered, for example, that there is no greater obstacle to mental health than the specific or exclusive determination to become healthy and remain so; in other words, the expressly proclaimed 'idea' of health is an obstacle to the 'reality' of health. On the subject of freedom, the general programme of the Congress states that not all ideas are conducive to freedom, and tells us to examine every idea from the point of view of how far it safeguards or endangers freedom. One might venture to say that the idea of freedom is itself one of the obstacles to the establishment of freedom. That is, of course, an exaggerated statement, which could easily be misunderstood and misinterpreted. But it is true, I think, to the extent that anyone who fights for the establishment of freedom must fight, first and foremost, for values which are determined by their inherent content (truth, justice, human dignity and so forth). And this applies to the Christian or religious resistance to tyranny of which we have documentary knowledge. I think the part played by implicit aims in the fight for freedom—even in the 'October' riots in Poland and in the Hungarian uprising—should not be underestimated. Paul Ignotus has told us here that the Hungarian resistance fighters were inspired largely by 'traditional' values. And in Hungary 'traditional' is probably synonymous with 'Christian'. Herbert Lüthy, too, said that Poland and Hungary were impelled not so much by nationalism as by the determination to establish a 'just form of society'; this again is obviously an inherent attitude.

It is admittedly very difficult—to the modern mind the essentially difficult problem—to discover the grounds for these inherent values and aims, express agreement with which constitutes, as I said just now, the true and perhaps the only preliminary condition for the achievement of freedom. For instance, authoritarian theory denies the rights of the individual, which are rooted in human nature; and that denial serves as the motive for withholding freedom. I believe that in intellectual discussions there is no way of reaching a solution except by demolishing this argument—in other words, by realizing (in the first place) that there really is such a thing as human nature (a point that is contested, for instance, in Sartre's existentialism; he declares that *Il n'y a pas de nature humaine*), and (in the second place) how and on what grounds this human nature confers on each individual human being—each partner in the human race—

certain unalterable, absolutely binding rights. It seems to me that it would be hard for anyone who cannot respond to this, to justify the demand for freedom.

Several speakers in our discussion have deplored the fact that people in 'the West', and especially university students, set little store by the idea of freedom. I wonder whether this alarming state of things may not be due to a failure to convince these young people of the significance and fundamental binding force of the *inherent* values on which the abstract concept of freedom can alone be based.

To put it briefly, it seems to me that the contribution of 'religion' to the achievement of freedom has taken two principal forms. In the first place, it has given names to those inherent values whose materialization brings freedom 'adventitiously' in its train; and in the second place it has supplied grounds and justification for those same values, whose binding power derives from a superhuman model.

Criticism and Discussion

KATHLEEN BLISS: . . . *no return to the simplicities of ignorance* . . .

Insofar as religions have been explanations of natural phenomena or ways of influencing natural events, they are bound to yield place to scientific knowledge and practice. All religions will in time encounter this adulthood of man. Now there seems to me to be more than one way of assessing the situation that we are in at present. It is often regarded as a long fought out battle in which, either gradually, or by a series of rapid engagements, religion has been expelled from one field after another; and this is seen as the heralding of the final defeat at the hands of an advancing science and technology. Either the problems of religion are solved in a different way, it is thought, or technology makes them unnecessary. On this view of things the religious person is the one who looks for gaps in human knowledge and fills them up with god-shaped explanations; or he is one who claims for prayer, that perhaps it will sometimes work where psychiatric treatment has failed; or perhaps in the last resort he is just someone who falls back on extra-sensory perception as a support for religious belief. I believe there is another way of evaluating this whole engagement leading to our present situation, namely that what has been happening has been not only the liberation of the mind of man or the exploration of the natural world, but also the liberation of religion itself. For religion has, for centuries, been used to explain every individual phenomenon. It has been also, in the form of codes and taboos, the social cement of many communities and it has always been in danger of being dragged down by popular ignorance into the world of superstition. All religions have had their prophets and the struggle of the prophets have always been with popular and debased forms of religion.

The task of the prophet is to recall man to religion in its highest form, an aspiration towards the love of the good and the

149

pursuit of it by hard endeavour. Now here perhaps we have to raise the question of the role of the religious institutions, a great stumbling block. Religious institutions always can be and frequently are the rallying point of every kind of conservatism. But I would also point out that without the religious institution, the prophet is comparatively helpless, for it is through the institution that he builds a following for his ideas and sets them into motion. The liberation of religion in the present situation seems to me to be the release we have obtained from the necessity of belonging to a society in which religion was stretched beyond its limits to everything in life. We now see more clearly that faith is a responsible act. This doesn't necessarily make it easier, perhaps the reverse, but it does make it clearly what it is.

To be in any genuine sense a religious person in the modern world demands, it seems to me, both intelligence and will. There is no return to the past, to the simplicities of ignorance, but there is an open possibility of reinstating our beliefs as those things to which we articulately submit ourselves.

One problem has greatly exercised freedom-loving parents: the upbringing of their children. It has been thought by many of them, that in order to respect their freedom, they must be brought up uncommitted in any ultimate belief. This has meant that, willy-nilly, parents have passed to their children the idea that commitment is somehow something to be avoided. We want above all things our children to be free; but it seems to me that to give them a vision of commitment, which, when adulthood is achieved, can be rebelled against, is a finer and, in the end, a more viable form of freedom in education, than a lack of commitment to anything but lack of commitment.

RICHARD HENSMAN: . . . . *a counterpoise to the authority of the State* . . .

It often happens that when the convictions that we live by are attacked or criticized by others we tend to get violently involved. Such feelings are likely to be so violent as to break the bounds of scholarly discussion and the taboo on religion today which Dr. Bliss spoke about has a cause which we should note at the outset: religious people have, in the past, not only been conservative; they have also very offensively interfered in the lives of others. They have been among the chief enemies of personal liberty. I myself believe that in some cases, in certain historical situations, a good dose of secularism and anticlericalism is a constructive and positive force in history and I believe this is true of my own country—Ceylon—at the present moment.

What, insofar as progress in freedom is concerned, are the present challenges and the present opportunities in the world as a whole?

When we think of small groups of economically and politically privileged people, then we can afford to see the virtues of moderation and rationality. But in the world as a whole, where life is a struggle and where resources are adequate only for a frugal and active life for all men, some men are tempted to live luxuriously by exploiting others. In fact in the greater part of the world the material pre-conditions of freedom don't exist.

We cannot discuss this subject without thinking about South Africa or China or Eastern Africa, where life seems to move, where much more fundamental issues of freedom are being raised than in the more ordered, more stable societies that we tend to talk about. Our main concern is with what religion claims to do and with what it is demonstrably able to do. I think the first point to be made about religious faith—and I refer specifically to Buddhism or Christianity—is that it is offered as a key to the emancipation of the self.

It is the essence of the higher religions that they define the state of men's life, of irreligious life, shall we say, as a state of ignorance about the fundamental facts of life and offer and recommend as a way of life, a way to realization of the self, and if we think of the personal life, of personal initiative, of personal responsibility as related to this release of the self, emancipation of the self, then here we have a clue, a pointer to what religion proposes to offer for the life of man in society under all conditions. My second point is that religion functions very often as culture of a group, as something that holds a group together. The authority which a religious group or religion offers, is something of a counterpoise to the authority of the community, the authority of the State.

At its best religion testifies to values and standards which are denied or ignored in society and in doing so it offers man a choice, an authority which he can place against what could be the very oppressive deadweight of the tradition of the community or the law of the State, the power of the State. On the other hand, of course, where you have religious hierarchies which claim allegiance over the minds of people, you have the situation which I referred to earlier: religion becomes an oppressive force.

HELMUT GOLLWITZER: . . . *This fortress of freedom* . . .

The universal claim to certain basic rights, which is included nowadays in the programmes of all governments, first arose out of the Christian doctrine of equality. Observation of nature, otherwise than as a branch of magic, originated with the Christian release of the world from its chains, and the debunking of magic.

The problem of reducing the tension between faith and knowledge has therefore a very different aspect within the Christian tradition from what it will now have for the Asian and African peoples with their own religions. One cannot foresee in what development of thought that will take place.

At one time there was a general tendency to assume that scientific and technical instruction would break up the historical religions. Somebody once said: 'By explaining to a Negro the working of a modern rifle, you do more to divorce him from his traditional heathen beliefs than through the preaching of all the missionaries put together.'

In fact, the contrary seems to be true. Self-awareness, among the Asian and African peoples, leads also to a strengthening of the old religions; they become adjusted, partly through the the incorporation of certain elements borrowed from Christianity such as the idea of loving one's neighbour. Christianity is felt to be the real problem, the soil from which secularism, materialism, Communism and so forth have sprung; but these peoples also recognize that there is something essentially 'different' about Christianity, and to some extent they turn in the opposite direction. In other words, I don't think Toynbee is right in saying that we are entering upon a period of smoothing out of the differences between the great world religions.

Mr. Hensman said that the value of religion was that it helped us to realize our true selves, and that it maintained and affirmed certain values which are denied or neglected in the present social order. This would mean that in any case the

Christian faith has the task of serving as a refuge for the truths that are forgotten or overlooked in each generation. But it seems important to me that we should realize that a de-humanizing influence can be exerted not only by want, hunger, slavery and the other characteristics of earlier ages which may be ultimately abolished in an affluent society. Affluence itself can be just as de-humanizing. The Christian contribution should therefore consist of the ideas derived from Christianity—the inalienable quality of man, the inviolability of conscience, the precedence of the individual over the species, the eternal value of the human soul. I say those ideas derive from Christianity, but someone may dispute this later on; in any case they have a very definite and, in my opinion, incomparable foundation in the basic tenets of the Christian faith. When they are divorced from the Christian faith and go into circulation as abstract ideas, they gradually lose their strength. So they have to be perpetually revived, and that is the responsibility of which Christians should always be reminding one another, in a world in which they see that certain ideas and categories of thought derived from the Christian tradition are spreading all over the earth in such an astounding way.

Anyone in the Communist world who is a Christian—and the same thing is very possibly true of Moslems, Buddhists and so forth, but I can only speak for the Christians—anyone in the Communist world who is a Christian is at once placed in a reserved area of freedom, in relation to the all-absorbing claims of the official ideology. He is bent upon widening the gaps in the ideological control system, upon recognition of the individual conscience; he indicts the conscience of the government officials, he is bent upon promoting individual responsibility, upon making the system less dogmatic and more human; his only hope, in earthly matters, is evolution, and he wishes to make an active contribution to it. Christians have learnt from their faith the conviction that man cannot be turned into an ant, even if the totalitarian systems try to produce that result; Christians in those countries no longer believe that; they themselves are a proof of the contrary, and they receive further surprising proofs of it every day.

The importance of religion in the fight for freedom lies in the fact that it protects the innermost core of man from the influence of every human power. During the Third Reich a friend of mine, a Bavarian parson, was visited by a peasant lad from his parish, who since he last saw him had joined the S.S. The lad explained that he was one of the guards of a concentration camp. The parson remarked that terrible things were said of such places, but the young man would not confide in him. And then suddenly he launched into another topic, saying that the S.S. were demanding that he should leave the Church; and he wanted the parson's opinion about that. 'You've hardly been inside the church since you were confirmed,' said the parson, 'so why do you feel any hesitation about leaving it altogether?' To which the young man replied, 'Well, the way I look at it, once they've got us outside the Church, they can do whatever they like with us.' By which he presumably meant: 'This very loose relationship to religion, my official membership of a congregation, is my last link with something higher than mankind, something that protects me from falling utterly into the power of men.' So I feel that we should look with sympathy upon this reserve of freedom, this fortress of freedom, into which religious-minded people can withdraw even under a totalitarian system. Inner freedom has often been contrasted with outward freedom, as though it were a consolation that could make people indifferent to outward freedom. But in fact, though inner freedom is naturally a consolation for the loss of outward freedom, it is also an incitement to fight for the cause of outward freedom.

JAYAPRAKASH NARAYAN: . . . *the unconquerable spirit of man . . .*

I have not been, in my life, professing any particular religion, but I have been concerned with both the question of freedom and the essence of religion. It is obvious to me, though I am not a student of religious history, that religions as they have been practised have in many cases acted as obstacles to freedom. I was born into the Hindu religion and, traditionally, Hinduism believes in caste and even in untouchability. That certainly is denial of freedom, restriction of freedom. Any religion, I think, which has a set of dogmas does restrict freedom of the mind, freedom of thought. Any religion which is based on organization, rigid organization, would necessarily restrict freedom. Any religion which would create a sort of hierarchy of religious beliefs would again limit freedom. At the same time, when I think of some of the highest concerns of Hinduism, which are freedom of the individual from all attachment, freedom from desires, freedom from the cycle of birth and death, then I think of Hinduism as a great liberating force. The Islamic religion or Christian religion speaks of the fatherhood of God and the brotherhood of men. That concept, if it is a religious concept, would again be a great force in the cause of freedom.

If all human beings are brothers, then no brother can deny or should deny freedom to another and that freedom will include all kinds of freedoms. Again, the way of love that Christ preached or the way of compassion that the Buddha preached, seem to me to be at the root of every kind of human freedom, material or spiritual. Therefore I should say that it is not easy to deal with the subject unless we are clear as to the terms we are using. In our struggle for freedom, for instance, in the Indian struggle for freedom, religion played a great role because it teaches the indestructibility of the human soul and those who were encouraged to participate in the freedom struggle were to be fortified by the belief that whatever the British did to them, they were indestructible and in that faith they became better fighters for freedom. Having won freedom it is quite possible that, as is happening in India, religion is used to oppress people. I cannot admit a religion that can divide human beings. Religion should be a uniting force. But the religions that exist today do divide the human family and I think this age of science and technology does demand a religion which would embrace the human race; the human beings lived far from one another, now they have been brought together into a small neighbourhood and any religion that acts as a barrier between them is, I think, an outdated institution.

I am not sure, in fact I doubt it very much, whether science alone can provide an adequate philosophy of life. I do feel that, if one is to fight for human freedom in all its forms, whether it is freedom from hunger or freedom of thoughts, freedom of the spirit, we have to go beyond science. We have often talked, I have myself talked about the unconquerable spirit of man, I don't know if science gives an evidence of this unconquerable spirit of man, but I have said it and I believe in it desperately, because if I give up that belief then I really become desperate about the future of the human race. I believe in this spirit of man and I do not think that this spirit would allow him to remain under oppression or would allow him to continue, as a human being. Now what is this spirit and how are we going to define it in secular terms, I do not know. This might bring us very near to religion, but even if we do not use the term I do not think that we can do without faith in this human spirit which seems to me beyond science and technology, beyond anthropology and sociology and psychology. It is this belief in the human spirit that really guarantees freedom, not only for today, but for always. Without this I do not think that it would be possible for us, rationally, to argue against the commissars and the planners and all those who are trying to give us the good things of our life.

SIDNEY HOOK: . . . *the legacy of Kant and Feuerbach* . . .

I shall take my point of departure from a remark made by my good friend Narayan when he said that he does not think that we could rationally justify our struggle for freedom unless we believe in the human spirit. I think I believe in the human spirit but it doesn't commit me to a belief in the existence of the soul which is a very disputed matter, and depends upon considerations not pertinent to the struggle of freedom. If we want to have a rational approach to this question, there are certain fundamental and perhaps elementary questions that one must ask oneself. Almost all of the speakers admitted that historically religion has often been opposed to freedom and quite specific freedoms, not general freedom in the way in which Professor Pieper discussed it, but freedom of inquiry, freedom of artistic expression, the kinds of freedoms which the Congress for Cultural Freedom believes in and wants to see expanded in the world. Now, if it is admitted that historically religion has often been opposed to freedom and if we say with Mr. Narayan that true religion ought to do this or that, isn't it obvious that the fundamental criterion becomes an ethical one and that you judge religion as acceptable or not acceptable, as good or bad, in terms of a criterion which cannot be derived from any religion since, by your own admission, the very same religion that you appeal to has in the past been used as historical justification for the caste system and discrimination. Now this, I think, is of tremendous importance because it raises the whole question of the relevance of religion to the struggle for freedom.

We know that Christianity never condemned slavery in principle, never condemned feudalism and that the first liberation movements were derived from the rationalist strain and stoicism. But I want to leave the historical evidence; sometimes religious movements have played a progressive role, sometimes they have not. It seems odd that in Berlin and in Germany, the legacy of Kant and the discoveries of Feuerbach are ignored. I come to the main analytical point: I ask the question of all of the speakers, who have shared the same generic point of view: show me specifically how you derive any concrete freedom from any theological or religious proposition? Of course if you are going to define religion in terms of passion or feeling, then everybody is religious unless he is half dead. But if you say that freedom depends upon the belief in the brotherhood of men and in the fatherhood of God, how do you get from the fatherhood of God to any particular, concrete freedom in this world? Because what is true for freedom, I should argue, is true for truth. The concept of truth cannot be derived from religion, because the validity of religion depends upon the acceptance of the value of truth.

After all it was Paul who said: 'All men are equal in the sight of the Lord, whether bound or free,' which indicates quite definitely for Paul and many who followed him that from the proposition that all men are equal in the sight of the Lord, it does not follow that they should be equal in the sight of the law or equal in some social respect. Not only India but the whole tradition of the West, up to modern times, indicated that one could be a good Christian believing in inequality, in other words that the belief in the fatherhood of God is compatible with any kind of a social system. And if someone tells me that this was a fallacy on the part of Christians in the past, I should answer that it is a little doubtful whether we can, for example, raise questions about the validity of the Christianity of Thomas Aquinas, who defends the death sentence, something which our Congress is opposed to. Consequently, the problem is to show the logical connection which is presumed to exist between religion and the struggle for freedom. I think that this connection must be established even if it were psychologically true that under some circumstances a belief in religion might inspire a belief in or a movement towards freedom. I submit that if we try to organize a struggle for freedom on the basis of religion, we divide our forces; sooner or later the question arises what is the true religion? Sooner or later we have to ask ourselves whether we can reconcile the different religions of the world.

INGEMAR HEDENIUS: . . . *the believer and the free thinker* . . .

The assumption that a logical relationship exists between religious beliefs and the belief in duty can only mean that I am being illogical if I say 'This is my duty, I am absolutely certain of that, but I doubt the existence of God, life after death, and so forth'. Whereas it seems to me that there is nothing at all illogical about asserting the one point—about duty—and denying, or expressing doubt about, the other. In my opinion, however, the question of logic is not interesting. There are other and more interesting questions that arise in this connection, such as psychological questions. For instance, does the believer in religion consider it necessary to be an ethical idealist—I mean, not only to talk like one, but to live like one as well? And it is perfectly clear that this psychological connection does not exist. So faith, in this sense, cannot be a necessary condition for ethical idealism—as is obvious from the fact that many free thinkers have proved themselves to be ethical idealists. Religious faith may of course be part of the basis for ethical idealism. And that, I think, is true, but it is only a platitude. There must be other contributory circumstances in addition to religious belief, such as courage, a certain zeal, the capacity not to be always thinking solely of one's own life, etc. In those circumstances religious belief may act as a powerful stimulus for ethical idealism. But the same can be said of agnostics and free thinkers, even of atheists. It obviously takes something more than agnosticism and atheism and so forth to make an ethical idealist. But the free thinker's conviction that we cannot hope for God's help in this life, or look forward to a future life, can also act as a powerful stimulus to ethical idealism. For it then becomes all the more necessary for us to make efforts on our own behalf, and that is a stimulus, too. In this sense, the believer and the free thinker are on the same footing. Neither has a monopoly of ethical idealism, both have equal rights in the matter.

KARL LOEWITH: . . . *only freedom can make us true* . . .

Dr. Bliss's paper did not convince me personally that the Christian belief, the injunction to love one's neighbour in the

Christian sense, has any essential connection with the 'Pursuit of Freedom', as it is called in the title. At any rate, not in the sense in which the Word 'freedom' is used in the American Declaration of Independence and in the French Declaration of Human Rights. I see no connection between the Christian claim that the cross takes upon it the suffering of the poor and humble, and what is known as secular materialism, the aim of which is to improve the lot of mankind through worldly means, redeem mankind through its own strength, and which consequently relies on the progress of science and technology. Christian freedom—this was implicit in what Mr. Gollwitzer said, too—is in essence a freedom from the world and all things worldly, and it presumably makes no fundamental difference to the believer in Christianity whether he is living in a totalitarian State or in a liberal democracy. And the statement that all men are equal, in the Christian sense, means only that they are equal in the sight of God—not before the law and among men, as men. But if we set aside this religious aspect, everything becomes different; what Christianity designates as 'sin' is seen as evil that will be got rid of by progress; the statement in the New Testament that only truth can make us free is reversed and becomes the statement that only freedom can make us true. 'Freedom from want, ignorance, disease, fear' is not a basic tenet of Christianity. I do not mean to suggest by all this that Christian freedom from worldly things cannot have constructive results, even in the worldly dealings of a Christian. It does, of course, have such results, as Mr. Gollwitzer's own observations indicate; but the preliminary condition for this Christian capacity to resist the so-called 'historical moment' is that, because of his faith, the Christian can stand aloof from other matters, in a way that is usually not possible for the non-believer.

Either we believe in science, in which case science must be allowed to have its say about human nature, or we turn to the New Testament for the answer to the question 'What is man'— and the answer we shall find there will not be the product of scientific reflection. I think it is essential for us to give up trying to find a more precise definition of what freedom is, or of the meaning attributed to it here; otherwise we shall be led into completely arbitrary inferences.

Criticism and Discussion

ENZO BOERI: ... *ignoramus et ignorabimus* ...

The Christian Church has opposed scientific inquiry from the very beginning, from the time of Galileo. It opposed all discoveries of geology and in the last century, all the discoveries of evolution. In a certain way, many of our discoveries which have led to the present civilization are more in the line of the pre-Christian than in the line of Christian tradition.

If I look from a more parochial point of view, in my country —Italy—religion is a very evident limitation to freedom. For instance, in our country former priests cannot teach in the schools, divorce cannot be legally obtained. If we look at the present religions in the world, be it the Christian, the Asian religions, the Jewish, any of them, they are all bound to privileges, to conservative positions, they have proved false in many occasions where they had to oppose with scientific thought. Nevertheless, we can well admit that there is an intrinsic religiousness of man and that some of the psychological problems of the present civilization are precisely due to the inadequateness of any religion in contrast with the intrinsic religiousness of man. Now what can be the way out of the present situation is very difficult to say. I should say that the most important thing is of course ethical code and, as for the problem of God, one hundred years ago a physiologist in this town said 'ignoramus et ignorabimus' and probably it is not the time to say 'ignoramus et non ignorabimus'.

ROBERT OPPENHEIMER: ... *freedom as an attribute of human life* ...

I have only something quite brief to say but it is addressed to Mr. Hook's plea that the Congress does not allow differences of attitude towards religion to interfere with its fundamental agreement on freedom. I cannot hear Professor Pieper or Mrs. Bliss speak without the deepest appreciation and admiration and I find myself close to what Mr. Narayan said. I think that it is true that we will never derive the great commitments of human life in an unambiguous way from religious doctrines. In a certain sense, they were not meant for that and I share Mr. Hook's despair when he attempts to do this. I do think, though, that there is an intermediate ground where we do have work to

160

do and that is in enlarging our agreement as to what we mean by freedom and what we hope for from it. When we mean freedom from tyranny, I think we are all in a simple, straight agreement and we are not very far from the things that we wish to see an end to. But when we talk of freedom as an attribute of human life, as something which we could hope would still be discussed a hundred years from now, we will, I think, share Professor Pieper's view that not all the good things in human life result from being aimed at; many are by-products and a discussion of the ways in which we would like to see the human spirit grow, is to my mind very much in order for the Congress for Cultural Freedom. To this those who are religious will bring a great deal and those who are agnostic will bring something too.

ALEX WEISSBERG: *. . . a totalitarian system of belief . . .*

Professor Pieper quite rightly differentiates between brutality resulting from actual theories, and brutality resulting from the misapplication of those theories. But in practice I think he is wrong in two respects—the case of the Christian Church and the case of Bolshevism. We can assume that Nazi totalitarianism acted in conformity with its theories. Everything that developed in course of time was latent in the ideas concerning race, the idea of the *Herrenvolk*, the maxim that 'whatever serves my nation is good and true'. But with Bolshevism it was different. The cradle of Communism was watched over by a deeply humanitarian idea, and the assault on freedom was committed only gradually and much against the will and against the feelings of the earliest Bolsheviks. Lenin believed that after three months of dictatorship people would realize that the Communists were right, and then there would be boundless, anarchical freedom. On the other hand, Pieper rather overshot the mark when he tried to clear Christianity from the obloquy of the Inquisition. We need not blame the Church for the excesses of the Borgias, for those were unchristian; but the attempt to create a totalitarian system of belief and admit of no division in it, right up to the Reformation, is entirely compatible with the basic tenets of the Christian Church. And in both cases the reason was the same: anyone who uses force in order to put over ideas that the majority of people don't want, or no longer want, must necessarily end by violating freedom. If Lenin's views had ever been

161

in harmony with the wishes of the great mass of the Russian people, those excesses would never have occurred. If, like the Church in the old days, a leader finds he can preserve the system—not only the system of power, but the way of looking at things—only by an assault on other people, then he commits the assault. When I came back from Russia and described how millions of people were being thrown into prison as profiteers and counter-revolutionaries, and that there was no kind of counter-revolutionary organization, that nothing of all that existed, people in England wouldn't believe me at first. So I said to them: Now look, in the course of three centuries in Germany, about 900,000 witches and wizards were burnt at the stake, but as we know nowadays there *were* no witches—just as there are no Trotskyites in Russia today. Later an English friend said to me, 'You're wrong, there *were* witches.' When I asked what he meant, he said: 'Not objectively, of course; because when those women believed they could make the milk go sour or set the crops on fire, they couldn't really do it. But they thought they could, and in that sense they formed an organization that people could join. So people who had turned to God and got nothing out of it might perhaps try the devil; and that meant just as dangerous competition for the Christian Church as heresy did, and that is why the full force of the totalitarian machinery of the Inquisition was directed against those alleged witches.' So we see that when a totalitarian power wants to maintain a system of thought or a system of power that runs counter to the true interests, or even merely to the opinions of the majority, it is compelled to use brute force.

RONALD SEGAL: ... *entrenched, organized religion* ...

I think that the speaker I heard defending the encouragement to freedom given by Christianity, on the other side of the Iron Curtain, would do well to consider what entrenched, organized religion is doing in the Union of South Africa where the Dutch Reformed Church, the nearest we have to an established church, is in fact peddling all the doctrines, all the dogmas of the repression. It is with considerable dismay that I have to report that one of the manifestations of political resistance in the Union today is now the burning of churches within African areas, and the burning not of Dutch reformed churches, but the burning of

Anglican churches and the burning of Catholic churches. Now, Mr. Chairman, this is a turning from religion that is not a regression towards tribalism which is the policy of the government itself, it is a running away from organized religion as the adverse side and the running away not from one sect but from all sects. It is perfectly true that on occasions other Christian sects in South Africa have opposed the peculiarly brutal stand taken by the Dutch Reformed Church, but the church of the province, which is the Anglican church in the Union, pays different stipends to white and to black, and within all the organized churches with European, American, international counterparts the senior hierarchy is entirely white. I have heard a great deal about the doctrine of love, the doctrine of compassion. In a society where it has been shown conclusively that compassion does not influence events, in a society where it appears increasingly every day that violence can only be met by some form of counter-violence, what stand can organized religion take? In a situation like in South Africa there is no religion at the moment in existence, no organized religion that can supply any of the answers to the very real problems that exist within a race-crazy society.

HUGH SETON-WATSON: . . . *a certain intolerance of the anti-clerical* . . .

In his *Origins of Totalitarian Democracy* Professor Talmon stressed the difference between intolerance and oppression in the name of something which is related to another life and intolerance in relation to the present world; the point that Talmon made was that when belief in another life ceased to operate, this led to an increase of intolerance, because once you believe that perfection can be achieved in this world, you have a duty to carry out this perfecting by any means available because the reckoning was not left to the next world but was here on this earth. And this led to a kind of intensification of oppression and intolerance. Now, I think there is something here, there is a connection between the disappearance of religion and totalitarianism. I do not by that mean that secularists or unbelievers as such are intolerant, but merely that the tendency towards intolerance and oppression and coercion of the mind and of the body which is present to some extent in all societies, has had a certain intensification as a result of the disintegration of religious belief, and the only reason why I want to mention this is to suggest that the argument isn't surely between those who say that you must be a believer in order to be in favour of freedom, or that you must be an unbeliever to be in favour of freedom. Surely we can stop this sort of sterile discussion which seems to me at times to have a kind of undertone of what I can only call old-fashioned nineteenth-century anti-clericalism. Of course there are parts of the world, we all know, in which religious intolerance is still very much in force; certainly in Spain, perhaps even in Italy, the power of the Church is still used to coerce men's minds. But it seems to me that tyranny is tyranny whether it is secularist or religious and we are against tyranny of either kind. I think it is still a widespread view and I seem to get echoes of it at times that there is something inherently tyrannical about religious belief. Now this seems to me to be utterly wrong. There is a certain intolerance of the anti-clerical towards religious belief as such which dates from the time in the eighteenth century when oppression and coercion of men's minds and bodies was in fact chiefly carried out by the Church and the Inquisition. In fact, religious belief does not necessarily lead to freedom but it does not necessarily lead to tyranny either.

Some Philosophical Remarks Concerning the Contemporary World

JEANNE HERSCH

THE text proposed to us by Mr. Polanyi referred to the 'hollow man'. It is that 'hollow man' I would like to talk about. For in my opinion this 'hollowness' constitutes a very great danger to the defence of the Western world and to what we mean here by 'freedom'. In his paper, Mr. Polanyi drew attention to a sequence of historical transformation which is important, but which is perhaps not the only one. I shall try to add certain features to those he pointed out to us.

It seems to me that at the heart of the question there is the radical disproportion, which colours our whole life nowadays, between the existence that the present day allows us, as individual human beings, and the tremendous power that is conferred upon us anonymously. I would like to begin by pointing out and commenting upon this disproportion.

It is a truism to say that science and technology have increased a hundredfold the power of the human being. Man, as such, at present wields a power beyond comparison greater than that which he possessed only forty years ago. That power entails a multiplication of our presence in the world, and a multiplication of the world's presence with us—through all the forms of information available to us, and which thrust themselves upon us whether we want it or not. For we are not free to take them or leave them alone. Nowadays, when there is a famine anywhere in the world, we hear about it, and we know approximately how many victims it has caused; we can no longer remain ignorant of it. The world is with us, as it were, in its entirety. And the fact of knowing about things means that we automatically feel some degree of responsibility for them. It seems to us that with the power we possess as human beings, we could prevent certain of the disasters that occur in the world, if we wanted to or if we knew how to set about it. This increased power thus entails an immense, perhaps exaggerated, increase in our sense of responsibility.

But at the same time our belief in progress has deserted us. After experiencing Hitler, after the crimes of that recent period, we believe we can attain to still greater power, we do not regard this as an unmixed blessing, as a definite sign that history is advancing along the right lines.

Moreover, at the very moment when his power and his presence were being thus multiplied, the human being has seen his specifically human qualities challenged as they had perhaps never been before. What Kant calls *die Menschheit im Menschen*, the humanity of man—the factors that make a human being human—has been called in question, to an increasing extent and in an ever more fundamental manner, by the biological sciences, and even more by the social sciences. These have striven, by a variety of methods and means, to reduce to a minimum the element in man which cannot be explained by casual relations, definable in terms of biological or social conditions. They have tried, as it were, to pare away man's irreducible core, in the apparent hope that finally there would be nothing left of him. Man would then be solely the product of his biological or social antecedents, and the causal chains linking all the facts of the universe would no longer be broken up by the effects of free will.

Science regards freedom as something negative, a point of non-explanation, a hiatus in the explanation. And *the present moment* is a kind of anomaly in the time of which science makes use—a time in which nobody is in any specific position, and which is assumed to be continuous. Science has done its utmost to get rid of the awkward exceptions constituted by freedom and by the present moment, which refuse to fit into the continuity that would make everything explicable. And the strange thing is that the social sciences, in taking this course, believed they were imitating the natural sciences, learning from them and in some way widening their frontiers: whereas it seems to me that in reality (I venture on this ground with great trepidation, especially considering some of those who are at present here)—it seems to me that on the contrary, by taking this line the social sciences have drawn further and further away from what

166

characterizes the natural sciences. For the latter have striven constantly for greater clarity in their methods; their standards of proof have been raised higher and higher and they have grown increasingly cautious in the interpretation of their results, their discoveries. Whereas the social sciences have been remarkable chiefly for the wide scope of the laws they laid down; the nice thing about these all-embracing laws being that they defied proof. In the natural sciences, the wider the application of a law, the more it requires to be proved; but in the field of social science, the wider the application of a law, the less the possibility of proving it. Generalization is here a definite convenience and one which the social sciences hardly ever seem to have resisted.

There has also been a trend which I might call existential. Perhaps driven to bay by the sciences which told him what he was and at the same time whittled away his essence as a free subject, man has, as it were, *withdrawn* from his explicable characteristics, those whose origin could be traced, and has concentrated more and more on the search for his irreducible self, the self belonging to him and to nobody else.

For instance, the nature of the individual was at one time determined by his *birth*. The term 'blue blood', as applied to the aristocrat, was not simply a metaphor; it meant that the very nature of the aristocrat differed from that of other people; and when a man was said *to be* an aristocrat the verb 'to be' had a very positive meaning. It meant that the property of being an aristocrat could not be removed from that man, that the fact of being one constituted his essential self, was an inseparable part of him.

Similarly, a man's *function* was an inseparable part of his nature; so that he had various attributes which clung to his nature, adhered to it, made part of it and combined to form it. King Lear, once he ceased to be a king, *ceased to exist*; whereas nowadays we have a whole crowd of dethroned kings who still exist. Even the function of royalty seems to us to survive without a peg to hang on; and the same applies to almost all functions, except perhaps that of the priest and—within the army itself, at any rate—that of the military officer.

It is the same thing with social *class*. In spite of what we are told to the contrary, the individual feels that his inner essence is something that transcends his class, and he tries to assert himself above and beyond his class, and finally comes to ignore it. It is the same, again, with *family status*. A father, for instance, is a man who happens to have a son. He is not essentially a father, someone who deserves respect, whatever he does, merely owing to his *being* a father. *Tradition*, even, is regarded as capable of effecting changes in the self, but not as being a substantial element of it. Self is something more than *character*, too— character seems to be only a contingent aspect of it.

This movement of withdrawal, by which the human being tries to grasp, by elimination, what is entirely essential and unique in him, his real self, has the ultimate effect of reducing that real self to a kind of abstract point, to the bare discontinuity of the passing moment, to the abstract inclusion of freedom in the causal chains I mentioned just now. We might quote here, with a different connotation, what Kipling says about the crab: '"I am I" says the crab, "myself and nothing else"' (not the exact words, of course—they're in one of the 'Just-So Stories') and recall Sartre's words, 'I am nothing.' Nothing that is to say, a break in the opaqueness of being.

Needless to say, this withdrawal of the 'self' automatically does away with the firm foundation on which society could build in former times, and which derived from the substantial, incorporated nature of the *symbols* on which human relationships were based. Those symbols were part and parcel of the person and its social relations, they were very little affected by the virtues, sentiments or necessarily shifting loyalties of individuals. They were supplied, as it were, both subjectively and objectively, at the same time as the social connections.

Now that this firm foundation has disappeared, we are confronted by a new situation. Either we must accept instability and capricious change, or we must resist, taking refuge in an impassioned moralism to which Mr. Polanyi referred the other day in a different context. From now on, in fact, the only prop for stability is the actual existence of the individual who takes a particular set of social connections as part of his life. The connections no longer hold by themselves, they depend on certain individuals.

Take the marriage bond, for example: so long as it is a sacrament, it is unaffected by anything that those who are connected by it may subsequently feel, think, experience or even wish; once it becomes personal it depends on the continuity of feeling of those individuals and on their behaviour. Personal freedom, when it withdraws out of any and every context in order to 'purify' itself and become 'inward' to the maximum degree, transforms all connections into something inward and personal. After that, any connection between persons is conditioned by the inner being of those persons.

It thus acquires a different and perhaps much greater value. It is not my intention here to weigh one against the other. But it is clear that once a connection withdraws inward, it immediately and inevitably becomes very fragile. The standard of morality based on firmly established precepts disappears, to be replaced (as can be very clearly seen, for instance, in recent French literature) by a single, very ill-defined value, which not only varies from one person to another, but may even fluctuate during the lifetime of a particular person: a certain demand for sincerity and authenticity.

The question then arises as to whether man can stand up to this kind of freedom, whether he can carry a burden so heavy. And is it to be hoped that society can be held together with that kind of freedom as its sole support? I think it should at any rate be realized that such freedom is something extremely difficult to take on. You remember the passage in Dostoievsky where the Grand Inquisitor declares that freedom is the most terrible gift ever bestowed on man; and it seems to me that this partly accounts for the lure of totalitarianism.

Please do not misunderstand me: I am not trying to defend one or the other way of being, or to censure either of them. But it seems to me that in the last forty years (though it would be easy to point to some far more remote periods) men have tried to take upon themselves a freedom, the risks and implications of which they failed to perceive beforehand. And then, as always happens, we were faced with the consequences, by life and by the facts.

I will turn now to another point. Now that, thanks to scientific and technical progress, man is no longer afraid of nature— having tamed the phenomena of nature—he has come to be afraid of another redoubtable nature that has risen up around him—of his fellow-man, of other men, of society, of history. For present-day man it is society and history that constitute the jungle, the unforeseeable, menacing, perilous territory. I think there has been a displacement of fear, with very profound consequences.

169

It is of course true that a network of security, lost at the beginning of the industrial era, has been reconstructed on the social level, chiefly owing to what is aptly known as 'social security'. But in my opinion the social security thus gained or regained, by strengthening people's desire to keep their place in the style of life and the environment where they can be sure of having it, has made them even more subject to the greater, more radical, lurking fear that threatens their *whole* security.

Man's relationship to history has become strangely equivocal nowadays. It is a master-slave relationship which works both ways and whose terms are interchangeable: history is the area of power, where a man's capacities and intentions find scope and his plans come to fruition; but conversely, history is the modern form of the doom that weighs down on him. Man enjoys history, but at the same time he would rather play no part in it, he wants to escape from it, he wants it to leave him in peace, to pass him by. He feels it to be subject to his plans, in other words malleable, yet at the same time all-powerful, fateful.

The same ambiguity is to be found in his relationship with the technological universe that now surrounds him, thanks to the advance of science. Man makes use of it every day, at every moment—he is continually using it, but without understanding *what* he is using. He is in the midst of a world that is submissive, but uncomprehended. So there revives, in the man of today, a receptivity towards superstitions, a tendency to be influenced by eschatological prospects and by escapist tendencies, and a vulnerability to immeasurable fears, which are in utter contrast to the feeling of power that is awakening in him. *Everything* seems possible, because hardly anything can be really understood. And the astonishing thing is that for us, who live in this great era of science, the part of the world that is really clear—the part we can all understand—is, proportionately speaking, extremely restricted.

Having become aware of history, willingly or unwillingly, consciously or unconsciously, man has to try to find a meaning for it. Attempts to do this are constantly being made on all sides. In present circumstances a philosophy of history thus seems to have become inevitable. On the other hand men, with the exception of great scientists, are usually devoured by impatience. They want to find the key at once, to know the last secret. Man finds it intolerable not to be told. He does not realize that the refusal to tell him the last secret makes part of the infinitely complex, fragile and precious balance which is among the components of human freedom. He thinks he might know how it ends and be free all the same—or be even *freer*, because then he would know what to do. This determination, this need, to discover the ultimate secret seems to me to be yet another factor that favours totalitarian propaganda in our midst.

But though the sense of history has become so keen among all our contemporaries (it is by no means the sole prerogative of the Marxists) it does not necessarily lead to political activity. Here we must realize something which is rather complicated but which seems to me to be important. To speak of history and to live 'historically' are two very different, in fact almost opposite, things. In talking about history one takes history as a kind of object, one holds it still in front of one. It is quite characteristic to find that, for instance, a philosophy of history such as Marxism gives us the *term* for it, thus transforming it into a thing, into a form of history which lies outside history.

So what all of us today need to do is to find our proper place between the meaning of history, our capacity for being present within it, the sense of our powers and our helplessness; all of which is very difficult to practise and take upon ourselves, for it is no mere theoretical result we have to achieve, nor is it a matter of tracing boundaries for neighbouring provinces. I think the question nowadays is not one of liking or disliking our time and its characteristics, but of really re-establishing contact with our time as it really is, with the possibilities it offers and the hope it allows—which is a different hope from that of other periods. This means that instead of asking ourselves whether the changes that have occurred are good or bad, we have to accept them and ask ourselves what we can make out of them. Mass media, mass culture and so forth are no longer things it rests with us to maintain or get rid of. What does rest with us, is the value we are to extract from them for the benefit of humanity. But while criticism is easy, invention is difficult. And invention is what is needed. Since these new media are there, we have to invent new methods.

I think it would be amusing to take an example that lies close at hand and say a few words about the methods of discussion in a Congress such as ours. A Congress like this, discussions like these, are also something new. We have assembled here from all the corners of the world because facilities for travel have become amazing, because we have microphones and simultaneous interpretation, and because all this enables us to talk together. Now it seems to me that such a meeting requires the invention of some method of discussion which has not yet been introduced. If I may make one or two suggestions, it seems to me that the first condition is that all the participants, irrespective of their rank, their qualifications, their past achievements, shall subordinate themselves entirely, unreservedly and without the least vanity to the interests of the progress of the discussion. That means recognizing our Chairman as a kind of conductor of an orchestra, whose baton we obey because it is he who has to ensure that the discussion proceeds smoothly. Secondly, the list of speakers should not be arranged according to the order in which they have applied to speak, because then one speaker can never reply to another, since each is always answering something said long before. On the contrary, I think, specific themes should be put up for discussion, and anything extraneous to the central theme should be mercilessly quashed. In saying all this I am not criticizing this particular Congress; all congresses are run in the same way nowadays. But I think it is a waste of our opportunities for *meeting* and being *present*, by confining ourselves to a long sequence of interventions, with no real debate, such as could have been just as well circulated by the good old-fashioned printing-press.

Another example: adult education. Here again, we must invent methods of continuing the education of adults, whoever they may be, whatever may be their occupation, throughout their lives. Science is advancing so rapidly, the world is changing so quickly, that it is nothing to have gone to school thirty or fifty years ago. So it is absolutely indispensable to keep on going to school throughout one's life. But that means inventing new methods, specially devised methods, for each different category of adults, so as to be able to start from what each of them does and knows already.

Only education of this kind can and must provide the first remedy for the absolutely crucial vice of the mass media, which is that they abolish all spontaneous activity and replace it by inert absorption. This, I think, is a fundamental problem. One of the participants in this Congress said the other day that he had learnt some most interesting things about the French abstract painter Manessier from a television programme. That is excellent, and there are undoubtedly some good programmes on television. But the question is whether, at the time of learning about Manessier, it was about Manessier that one *wanted* to learn. The question is, where the personal interests of the person watching television lie, and whether those interests should be stimulated or, on the contrary, weakened or even destroyed and replaced by a colourless apathy, a void to be filled. It is essential that the impetus should continue to come from people, not from the machines; so it is imperative to intensify interest, and a selective faculty arising from that interest. And this, too, requires new educational techniques.

My reason for running so quickly through these examples is not that I consider them unimportant, but for lack of time, and because I cannot resist making a few more suggestions, though they are perhaps already too numerous and disjointed. Here is another: I think we should *prefer the workshop to the salon*, creativeness to finished perfection. Our generation has developed a worship of perfection, especially in art, which is on the way to killing culture. It is a good thing for certain programmes to be flawless, but there must be room left for practice, for growth, for spontaneity as well. When one eats fresh fruit one always finds some bad ones in the lot. When you eat tinned fruit you can be certain they will all be magnificent. But the difference is the difference between what is fresh and what is canned. And it is the same thing with culture. One must run the risk of failure, in order to produce something that is alive. What I mean by the salon is the place where you assemble everything you consider perfect; what I mean by the workshop is the place where one tries to *make* something, which may end either in failure or success. We have to take the risk.

I would like to seize the chance, now that I have the floor, to make a few more comments on the papers we have heard in the last few days.

As to political and economic matters, there is only one thing I want to say—that we have to devise socialist and federalist structures that will make possible that *dispersion of power* that Mr. Narayan, for one, spoke of the other day in our sociological study-group.

Concerning the religious question, I think that that, too, has changed its aspect, in a world so profoundly transformed. And

I would like to point out, for one thing, that when people begin to ask questions, as we have been doing here, about the possible value of faith in a world such as that of today, either in a country's development or in the education of its children, or for the purposes of some other result which in itself is excellent, it means that, without realizing it, they are already opting against faith. I do not want to go more fully into this idea, but I think it is fundamental. One is not really talking about faith unless one understands that.

Another point raised was whether religious faith was compatible with freedom. From the angle of freedom, and from a standpoint outside faith, one can only judge religious *institutions*. One may ask whether a particular religious institution promotes freedom or militates against it. But one cannot ask whether faith promotes freedom, because for those who have faith, faith and freedom are one and the same thing.

Then I think that the distinction between the category of 'believers' and that of 'unbelievers' is no longer as clear-cut as it may have been in other epochs. I want to make it clear that I am not trying to blur the outlines in order to bring everybody into agreement. On the contrary, I realize that there are believers and unbelievers. But I think that the quality has some resemblance to the 'uncertain halo' of which Schwarz-Bart speaks in *Le Dernier des Justes*. Those of you who have read the novel will remember that in the Lévy family, whose story it relates, there was one just man in each generation. But a time came when no one was absolutely certain who he was. And Schwarz-Bart tells us that from then on, in the Lévy family, the halo became a kind of question-mark, for no one was sure behind whose head it was placed. This idea of a suspended halo expresses more or less what I think about the distinction between believers and unbelievers.

As long as we are dealing with the subject simply on the level of external, theoretical discussion, the distinction is of little consequence. But when it comes to freedom, I feel—but this is my personal conviction, which I offer, of course, for discussion —I feel that freedom loses its meaning once all species of transcendence, that is to say, all species of reference to reality which transcends the practical sphere, is abolished. I think that when we reduce reality to mere immanence, history is reduced to a technical composition. And to know what to do in a technical composition, one must be an engineer. So in that case it becomes logical and sensible to entrust history to engineers. But I think pure immanence is an error, and precisely for that reason there are not and cannot be any engineers properly equipped to build history. That is why—and here I come back, after wandering so far, to my original theme—pure immanence, in my opinion, cancels out the actual, living present. It restores the objective continuity of time, which is nobody's time. It abolishes the decisive link between a past which has occurred and a future which is unknown—the link constituted by the present moment, that instant in which freedom can live.

Criticism and Discussion

SIDNEY HOOK: ... *a naturalistic view of man* ...

The paper of Madame Hersch has an aesthetic quality which is extremely attractive and I hesitate to raise certain difficulties of an analytical character with it, but I am sure she would understand that I feel I should do less than justice to her contribution if I did not ask for more light. My first question is whether or not she has distinguished clearly between different conceptions of freedom which she uses interchangeably here and which makes it very difficult for some of us to understand. She speaks of freedom in one sense as opposed to determinism; she identifies freedom in some places with discontinuity, freedom with chance. This is the old traditional question of freedom versus determinism and I, for one, do not see its relevance at all to the second conception of freedom, which is freedom from coercion, freedom from the arbitrary imposition of someone else's will. No matter what theory one has about determinism, or about chance —and one can raise certain philosophical difficulties with the view that has been taken in relation to that—they are not relevant to the question of the conditions under which human beings can express what they desire; how to abolish tyranny over the human mind. One can hold the same views of determinism and come to different conclusions about the nature and even the validity of coercion. If a man holds my hand and prevents me from moving, he is coercing me; if he lets me go, he is not coercing me. Now in either case, those who accept the postulate of determinism would say: the action is determined. But the determinism of those actions does not bear upon the question of whether a man should be coerced, of whether we agree with Hobbes or whether we agree with Mill, both of whom were determinists but who stood at opposite ends of the political spectrum. And I find a third conception of freedom and liberty here which I, for one, cannot connect with either one of the other two; in speaking of religious faith, Madame Hersch tells us: 'Faith for those who have it *is* liberty.' Now this, of course, sounds like a very arbitrary definition, but on what conception can one derive a theory of liberty which identifies it with faith, with spontaneity and with freedom from coercion? I think these three concepts are logically independent of each other and do not shed light on the subject. Certainly Augustine had faith, Paul had faith but I wouldn't say they have faith in liberty in a sense in which we are fighting for liberty today; a man might have faith and still not believe in liberty. My second point is one in which I can express a considerable and cordial measure of agreement with Madame Hersch. She says that it is necessary in our time to invent new methods of education, new methods of distributing power, new methods of creativity in life.

I thoroughly agree. I call that the process of creative intelligence. But to do that, we have to bring to bear some of those powers which I'm afraid have been criticized in terms of engineering; invention is very close to engineering. She seems to be calling for a method of social engineering. Now, I don't like the word 'social engineering' because it is a jest, implying that when we deal with social affairs we are dealing with material that can be assimilated to the things in the physical world and that we are going to treat human beings as if they were so much cement and metal and so on. But if we look away from that simplification, the essence of the application of methods of creative intelligence is the extension of this scientific method which is based, if I understand the word, upon the immanence of man. Now I should like to ask: Precisely why does it follow that if one believes that man is immanent in nature one cannot believe in liberty? Obviously man can believe in transcendence and deny liberty. We might refer to the existentialist theologians who continuate a long and venerable tradition and who tell us that from the transcendental conception of man both good and evil are equally irrelevant. Kierkegaard, in *Fear and Trembling*, when he discusses the Abraham-Isaac legend, calls attention to the fact that a transcendental view must lead to what he calls a suspension of the ethical. He says that from the standpoint of the absolute and the transcendent, Abraham acts like a murderer. But he maintains you cannot judge him, or if you judge him from a moral point of view then you are not judging him from a religious point of view. Karl Barth, his modern disciple, tells us that God loves Stalin and Hitler just as much as he loves their victims. Well, that tells us something about Karl Barth perhaps more than about God. But it is quite clear to me that in the sense in which we are concerned with freedom from coercion, which is the basic political issue, it has to be proven and not merely asserted that one who takes a naturalistic view of man on the basis of the only reliable knowledge that we have, has no right to believe in freedom.

JEANNE HERSCH: ... *freedom experienced by the individual* ...

I will try to reply to Mr. Sidney Hook, but that is extremely difficult, because what he talked about was worlds apart from what I tried to talk about. We both want more light, of course; but light is not always what people imagine it to be. And sometimes there may be clarity in the foreground of certain ideas, yet that very clarity may conceal the darkness that lies behind. There is sometimes a screen of clarity that conceals the truth. And it seems to me that the terms you use form a kind of screen of clarity which conceals a sort of gaping void that lies behind them, instead of shedding light on it. And those dark depths are of great importance in our life. I will take your questions and do my best to answer them.

You began by saying that I ought to have drawn a distinction between three types of freedom—the freedom that is spontaneity, the freedom that is absence of coercion, and the freedom which, for the believer, is indistinguishable from faith. You challenge me to explain in which of these three senses I was using the word 'freedom'. The fact is that I wasn't using it in any of those senses. I was speaking of freedom *experienced*. Freedom observed as spontaneity, from outside, *appears* to be a choice; but that is not what I meant. I meant freedom as experienced by the individual, nothing else. Regarded from outside, such freedom *appears*, I think, as an interruption in the determinist explanations. It is not *experienced* as such. Kant, of course, was quite right in affirming that the determinists are perfectly entitled to investigate the new phenomenon which *appears* after this break in continuity and try to reduce it by causal explanations. That is a perfectly legitimate undertaking, but it does not get rid of the break in continuity, which is caused by the very presence of freedom. I was in no way referring here to political freedom, that is to say, to freedom as absence of coercion. I assure you I often think of it. But today I took my stand on the ground which in my opinion makes necessary, and justifies and feeds, the struggle for the preservation of the form of freedom which is constituted by the absence of coercion. On the political plane, where freedom consists in the absence of coercion, it is merely *absence*—as you very rightly said. And one cannot fight solely for an absence. So that absence must have a substantial meaning somewhere or other. And that is what I tried to talk about.

As for what I said about the believer's identification of faith with freedom, you think that is an arbitrary definition. But it is not a definition at all. It would be absurd to define freedom in terms of faith, for the very good reason that there is no word more difficult to define than 'faith'. All I said was (and without giving it as my own view, because to do that would have been to arrest the wandering halo I spoke of; so I did not say that *for me* faith and freedom were one and the same thing) that *for the believer* who speaks from within his faith, the question 'Does faith contribute to freedom?' is meaningless, because he regards the two as absolutely identical. Or rather, as one and the same thing. That was all I said. And I cannot go further into it, for the matter at issue is the situation of the believer, and it seems to me that even he himself can hardly talk about it. You raised the objection that in the case of St. Augustine faith did not mean faith in freedom. I never said that faith necessarily meant faith in freedom. I said that for those who have faith, the heart of faith and the heart of freedom are one and the same thing. That's all. One can, of course, have faith and not live in freedom. But when one does not live in freedom, but has faith, there probably remains a spark of freedom which is intangible, and that is just what Socrates was referring to when he was dying, for instance. And that is what all those who had faith have referred to—lashed to a post and declaring that all the same, they were free. It would be an abominable sophistry, of course, to make out that since, whatever happens, that ultimate freedom remains intangible, there is no point in fighting for freedom on the political level. That would be the worst of spiritual operations, the worst abuse. But the possibility of such an abuse does not prevent that last spark from having its meaning, and perhaps even a meaning that carries all the others with it.

Referring to new methods, you said that invention is closely related to engineering. I know so little about the world of machines that I am almost afraid of talking about it. But it seems to me that if engineering is closely related to invention, it is precisely because it involves an element of invention which is truly creative, not merely a change in the positions of manufactured parts. In that sense, it is true, it is the same thing. In so far as invention plays a part in engineering (and it undoubtedly does), they are the same thing. But the 'engineer' as I used the word means someone who, as the Marxists put it, 'holds the key to history'. For such men history has no more mystery, no more secrets; their explanations exhaust its reality and consequently exhaust the reality of man and his life. If anyone can really master such knowledge, we need only leave it to him to arrange things for the best, with no interference; and it would be unreasonable not to accept the domination of such an engineer. But what I was talking about was the *meaning*, which evades learning, science and technique—and which in any case already lies at the heart of science and technique, as part of the reason why we *prefer* the true to the false. The preference for truth as against falsehood is not scientific. It underlies science, but it is not scientific. The impulse towards the truth is not scientific. And in my opinion that irreducible root is indispensable if we are to preserve the meaning and the place of freedom.

You asked me why I linked transcendence with freedom and immanence with loss of freedom. As a matter of fact I have already answered that point, because your third question is more or less the same as your second, perhaps even as the first. Because the same thing lies at the centre of all these questions, doesn't it? You quoted, from Kierkegaard and from Barth, two sentences which I agree seem particularly shocking at a first glance. But I would be ready to take up the defence of those two sentences, to make a commentary on them, and I think I could justify them. For if we leave God his divine mystery and if we leave the term 'love' the mysterious sense it takes on when applied to God, the words 'God loves the Nazis as much as their victims' is not only justified but indispensable. In any case Karl Barth's past entitles him to write such things, for it rules out any possible ambiguity.

RAJA RAO: . . . *where is freedom if not in transcendency?* . . .

I hate to remind you that I come of a civilization which has a certain wisdom and a certain stability, so that we can speak with a certain impartiality. For us in India, freedom means liberation —freedom is a process, liberation is its conclusion. The conclusion of what? Can one really be free when one still has a body?

Mr. Hook spoke of physical coercion; so it begins with the physical world, the world where one has a body; after that we come to the psychological world, which is conditioned, as Mr. Hook is conditioned, as we are all conditioned. So where is freedom, if not in transcendency, of which faith is a kind of popularization?

Freedom is the very heart of faith, which I will call the light that irradiates faith—that is what it is. I am in full agreement with Madame Hersch, I think, in saying that unless human beings can see themselves and see what is the nature of true freedom, which is transcendency, man will never be free.

I would like to ask Madame Hersch, is not the real question in the West, that there is a real, metaphysical conflict between antiquity and Christianity? I think that until that conflict is settled you will always have philosophers, you will always have nihilism.

JEANNE HERSCH: . . . *there will always be philosophers* . . .

I would like to thank Mr. Rao. I think there is one extremely important point on which I cannot agree with him. This is the question of the body. He wonders how one can be free when one has a body. I personally, as a good Westerner, would like to ask how one can be free when one hasn't got a body. For me, one of the characteristics of Western thought is that it is linked with the body—'a soul in a body', as Rimbaud says. I don't know what freedom without a body could be like. I don't say it doesn't exist; but for me, it passes human understanding. That, of course, leads to great divergence between your ideas and mine.

You said that so long as the conflict between antiquity and Christianity continues, there will always be philosophers and there will always be nihilism. I'm going to make a confession: I hope there will always be philosophers and that there will always be nihilism. For I hope there will always be faith and life, and there can only be faith and life while there is nihilism, and philosophers, and problems, and dramas, and difficulties. And it seems to me that the difficulties are due to the very fact that the plane Mr. Hook spoke of—the political plane, where freedom has to have elbow-room to exist without coercion—is by no means divided from the plane I myself spoke of. In my opinion neither of those planes can exist without the other. And the one on which I took my stand today in order to talk about freedom becomes quite artificial unless it is *also* slanted towards political action, in order to bring about on the social plane that absence of coercion to which we have referred.

A Postscript
MICHAEL POLANYI

ON returning from his meeting with Krushchev, held over the first week-end of June 1961, President Kennedy reported:

> 'The facts of the matter are that the Soviets and ourselves give wholly different meanings to the same words: war, peace, democracy and popular will. We have wholly different views of right and wrong and what is an internal affair and what is aggression. And above all, we have wholly different concepts of where the world is and where it is going.'

How did we get here and where do we go from here? This was, in effect, the question I put to the meeting in Berlin, a year earlier, by asking them to discuss my paper 'Beyond Nihilism'.

Confronted with this question, people think first of the impact of industrialization. But sitting as we did in the Congress Hall of Berlin, a few hundred yards from the Brandenburg Gate—which marks the frontier between the two halves of the world dominated by the two different systems of ideas—it was obvious that their disparity would not be explained by differences in industrial development. There is no great difference in this respect on either side of the Brandenburg Gate, and what is more, there is no difference in the degree or history of industrialization of the 'Federal Republic of Germany' under Adenauer and the 'German Democratic Republic' under Ulbricht. Industrialization may offer an opportunity for the spreading of new ideas, but it neither produces them nor lends them power to convince men.

The immediate reason for the dominance of distinctive ideas all over the eastern zone of Germany is obviously the presence of some twenty divisions of Russian troops ready to uphold the Communist government against the opposition which would otherwise have swept it away along with the whole system of distinctive ideas which it imposed on its people.

But this cannot either be the root of the matter. It leaves unexplained how the power of Communist governments originally came into existence at the centres from which it subsequently spread to other parts of the world. And it leaves unexplained also how a system of ideas, in many ways similar to that of Communism, had established, less than twenty years earlier, the equally oppressive rule of National Socialism all over Germany.

We must face the fact that these disasters of the twentieth century were primarily brought about by groups of fanatics who gained influence over broad masses. We must recognize indeed that these ideas so different from our own, which President Kennedy met with in Vienna, are still echoing throughout the planet and still gain adherents, particularly among the more educated people. We must acknowledge that these people embrace these ideas with fervent hopes for humanity, dedicated to fight for them and to suppress any opposition to them.

The main difficulty in understanding the power of modern totalitarian ideas is the habit of thinking of them in terms of the conflict between progress and reaction. They are not part of the struggle that has dominated men's minds since the Enlightenment shattered Christian dogmas and the French Revolution shattered feudalism in Europe. The revolutions of the twentieth century are not in line with this conflict. They do not aim at restoring either the dogmas or authorities against which the Enlightenment and the French Revolution fought. They are dogmatic and oppressive in an entirely new way which—by a strange logical process—assimilates for its purposes the great passions of scepticism and social reform which first achieved free thought and popular government in Europe and America.

The biography of Karl Marx by Isaiah Berlin has a passage which reveals this transmutation. It reads:

> 'The manuscripts of the numerous manifestos, professions of faith and programmes of action to which he [Marx] appended his name, still bear the strokes of the pen and the fierce marginal comments with which he sought to obliterate all references to eternal justice, the equality of man, the rights of individuals or nations, the liberty of conscience, the fight for civilization and other such phrases which were the stock in trade ... of the democratic movements of his time; he looked upon these as so much worthless cant indicating confusion of thought and ineffectiveness in action.'

Why did Marx so fiercely obliterate all references to justice, equality and freedom from his manifestos? Because he believed he had far better, more honest and intelligent grounds on which to achieve these aims. He had written:

> 'It is not the consciousness of human beings that determines their existence but conversely it is their social existence that determines their consciousness.'

To him, therefore, the revolution which would transform the existence of society became the primary aim and a true embodiment of his demand for righteousness. Even his own resolve to fight for this revolution was disguised in the form of a scientific sociology which predicted its inevitable approach, by virtue of its immensely increased productive capacity.

Such an ideology simultaneously satisfies both the demands for scientific objectivity and the ideals of social justice, by interpreting man and history in terms of power and profit, while injecting into this materialistic reality the messianic passion for a free and righteous society.

The potency of this combination has its counterpart in the weakness of the position confronting it: the position that we ourselves are trying to uphold. Our scientific outlook conflicts with our moral convictions, as it denies their objective justification. Our most fervent beliefs falter on our lips as their authenticity is questioned by our critical powers. Words like those of Woodrow Wilson invoking the conscience of world opinion, which once aroused Europe, sound hollow today. Our intellectual conscience has driven our moral convictions underground. But these antinomies which make the liberal mind stagger and fumble, are the joy and strength of Marxism: for the more far-flung are our moral aspirations and the more severely objectivistic is our outlook, the more powerful is a combination in which these contradictory principles mutually reinforce each other. We must face the fact that our own ideals, though true and right, are cramped by an internal conflict and tortured by a self-doubt which our opponents have eliminated, by embodying their moral aspirations in a scientism which defines their own power as the ultimate goal and moral purpose of mankind.

Some contributors to the discussion of my paper have called this hypocrisy. It is actually the inverse of it. Hypocrisy conceals lust for power behind a screen of moral professions; but Bolsheviks silence their moral aspirations and identify them with an unconditional support of Bolshevik power. They may sometimes sound sanctimonious, but their strength lies in being frankly hardboiled. An analysis of the chief propagandistic writings of Lenin and Stalin shows that ninety-four to ninety-nine per cent of the references to the Communist Party and its activities describe it as seizing, manipulating and consolidating power.[1]

This, surely, is the inverse of hypocrisy. Its spearhead is indeed to accuse our own society as hypocritical, for professing ideals of truth, liberty and justice against which it often offends —and cannot help offending. I have described therefore the structure of Marxism as a form of 'moral inversion' and under this label I have classed it with other mentalities which have a similar structure and are, moreover, rooted in the same historical antecedents.[2] This kinship has been criticized in the discussion, as if it identified the political types linked by kinship. But elephants and whales are both mammals and yet quite different animals. Marxism and Nazism are also very different, even though they have a similar structure and spring from common origins. Their kindred structures have different contents; Marxism is a revolutionary utilitarianism, Nazism a revolutionary romanticism. But their seductivity is of a similar kind; it lies in offering paths of intense political action to men estranged by a moral rebellion armed with moral scepticism, a combination which I have equated—not without historical reasons—with nihilism.

I must digress here to impress on the reader that I have not invented the problem which I am trying to solve here. Many authors have seen it. It was brilliantly introduced by Roger Callois.[3] Marx and Engels, he says, built up their formidable theory for

---

[1] See G. A. Almond: *The Appeals of Communism*, Princeton 1954, p. 22.

[2] 'Moral inversion' can be understood as a counterpart to Freudian 'sublimation'. 'Sublimation' designates the (alleged) transmutation of sexual libido into nobler manifestations of the mind, while moral inversion refers to the opposite transmutation of noble ideals into a quest for power and profit. Accordingly, I regard Freud's theory of sublimation as an expression of the same reductionist urge pervading our modern mentality, which, consistently applied, led to moral inversion.

[3] Roger Callois: *Description du Marxisme* (Gallimard, 1950).

188

the purpose of concealing from themselves and others that they were following the voice of their generous conscience, instilled by an education which their theory unmasked as fundamentally hypocritical. They transmuted their moral demands by uttering them in the form of scientific predictions. J. Plamenatz[1] struggled with the same paradox and concluded "'Scientific socialism" is a logical absurdity, a myth, a revolutionary slogan, the happy inspiration of two moralists who wanted to be unlike all moralists before them.' H. B. Acton[2] examines this logical absurdity and hints at the origins of its convincing power: 'The Marxist can derive moral precepts from his social science . . . to the extent that they already form, because of the vocabulary used, a concealed and unacknowledged part of it.' Carew Hunt[3] reveals this practice in the following quotation from Lenin: 'Morality is what serves to destroy the old exploiting society.' The struggle for power is set up here as the ultimate criterion of morality in words justifying this struggle by a moral condemnation of capitalism. The period of pre-Marxist Russian nihilism in which moral passions were first embodied in the revolutionary struggle for power is described by E. H. Carr[4] in his biography of Bakunin. It was Nechayev, around 1870, who took the final step of abandoning the romantic aspirations of the previous generation and raising revolution to the status of an absolute good, overriding any moral obligations. The ensuing internal contradiction is analysed for Russian Marxism by Bochenski.[5] Moral laws, he says, are appealed to and then it is denied that any such laws exist. In describing the militant mentality of the Soviets, Richard Lowenthal reveals its contradictions in paradoxical terms. He speaks of an 'unconscious and indeed fanatical hypocrisy—[a] ruthless immoralism justified by the subjectively sincere belief in the millennial rule of saints.' But how can hypocrisy, which is a pretence, be fanatical? And how can it be also an immoralism—that is, an open denial of the ideas invoked by hypocrisy? Lowenthal joins issue with me for rejecting the current description of the Soviet mentality as a 'secular religion'. I regard this term as misleading for it

[1] John Plamenatz: *German Marxism and Russian Communism* (1954), p. 50.

[2] H. B. Acton: *The Illusion of an Epoch* (1955), p. 190.

[3] R. N. Carew Hunt: *The Theory and Practice of Communism* (1950), p. 80.

[4] E. H. Carr: *Michael Bakunin* (1937), p. 376.

[5] Bochenski: *Der Sowietrussiche Dialektische Materialismus* (1950), p. 156.

might equally apply to any fervent patriotic or social movement forming part of the liberal tradition which is the primary opponent of Communism.[1] The problem I want to face was clearly formulated by Hannah Arendt:[2] 'Bolshevik assurance inside and outside Russia that they do not recognize ordinary moral standards have become a mainstay of Communist propaganda . . .' An attempt to explain why this concealment of moral purpose behind professions of immoralism is so stable and seductive has recently been made by E. E. Hirschmann:[3] 'We must realize that this disregard [of humanitarian idealism] has been a source of strength not of weakness. For because men in their moral professions have for so long not meant what they said, because the moral will has not seemed a reality which men could trust, therefore, by seeming to depend less on moral profession and moral will, they seemed the more to mean what they said and the more to rely upon realities.' Mr. Hirschmann sees a kindred tendency underlying 'the greatest self-conscious assault on humanitarian ideals yet seen in history, that of the Rome-Berlin-Tokyo axis'. Nearly forty years earlier Meinecke[4] had interpreted the tragic failure of imperial German mentality as due to the idea that the only true morality of a nation was

---

[1] The 'famous speech at Amsterdam on September 8, 1872' to which Lowenthal refers as contradicting my statement that for Marx violence was the proper aim of a scientific socialism is famous only because it is at variance with the most emphatic statements of Marx to the contrary:

'The Communists disdain to conceal their views and aims. They openly declare that their ends can be attained only by the forcible overthrow of all existing social conditions. Let the ruling classes tremble at a Communistic revolution.'

This peroration of the Communist Manifesto was a million times more effective as Marx's teaching than his speech in Amsterdam saying that in certain cases socialism could be achieved constitutionally.

Lowenthal says that Marx has drawn up fairly precise outlines for his own Utopia. The only text I can think of consists of a few vague pages in the 'Critique of the Gotha Programme' written as a letter to Bracke—of which Engels found a copy among his papers in 1891, nine years after the death of Marx. On the eve of the Russian Revolution Lenin could find no other Marxian basis than this document left unpublished for sixteen years—first by Marx and then by Engels—for shaping the programme of the future society in *The State and Revolution* (1917).

[2] Hannah Arendt: *The Burden of our Time* (1951), p. 301.

[3] E. E. Hirschmann: *On Human Unity* (1961), p. 124.

[4] Meinecke: *Die Idee der Staatsraison* (1929), *passim*. Immanence is also called here 'Monismus' and related to Hegel's 'Identitätslehre'.

immanent in its will to power. I think one could use the term 'immanent morality' instead of 'inverted morality' and I have occasionally done so. But 'immanence' lacks the terrifying overtones of 'inversion', as a state in which moral passions are transmuted into the hidden fuel of absolute violence.

The morally inverted mentality can be individualistic, un-political—this I call nihilism. In my paper, 'nihilism' means neither moral depravity nor moral indifference. Depraved in-dividuals have often joined company with modern nihilists and become instruments of the revolutions of the twentieth century. But by themselves they could have only produced a crime-wave —not made revolutions. Their mentality is poles apart from that of the personage first identified as a nihilist by Turgenev in his hero Bazarov. This character, which has made history, represents the rebellious Russian intelligentsia of the 1860's who repudiated all existing bonds of society in the name of an absolute utilitarianism, of which they hoped that it would liberate men and make them all brothers.

The romantic nihilism first propounded by Nietzsche in Ger-many, was likewise a moral protest against existing morality. 'This shop,' writes Nietzsche, 'where they manufacture ideals seems to me to stink of lies.' In place of this hypocrisy he sets the noble ideal of 'something perfect, wholly achieved, happy, magnificently triumphant, something still capable of inspiring fear'. He finds it represented in Napoleon, 'that synthesis of the brutish with the more than human'.

The beginnings of a nihilism associated with moral protest go back further. Diderot speaks of it already in 1763 in *Le Neveu de Rameau* whose immoralism justifies itself by the hypocrisy of society. Soon after, Rousseau made a monumental declaration of moral independence in his *Confessions*, exhibiting his vices as nature's naked truth. And later in the century the Marquis de Sade gave an account of his cruelty and lust, de-riving intellectual and moral superiority for his acts from a scientism which reduces man to a machine and a political theory which denounces laws as the will of the stronger.

Owing to its moral and intellectual appeal, nihilism has served as a cultural leaven throughout the past two centuries. A rebel-lious immoralism has bred the modern *bohémien* in France and the disaffected intellectual throughout the continent of Europe, and these alienated groups have contributed decisively to the

191

renewal of art and thought since the second half of the nine-teenth century. In this cultural process the two kinds of nihilism, the 'utilitarian' and the 'romantic', were interwoven. But I shall pick out one thread of the latter kind which leads us back to the social and political scene and to the romantic branch of modern totalitarianism. The movement which in France produced the *bohème* and in Russia the revolutionary intelligentsia, found an even wider outlet in the German Youth Movement. From small beginnings at the end of the nineteenth century, it came to comprise millions of boys and girls by the end of the First World War. At a famous congress on the Hohe Meissner Mountain in 1913, it dedicated itself to a fervent 'inner truthfulness,' condemning existing morality as a bondage im-posed by a corrupt society and affirming instead the romantic values idealized by Nietzsche, Wagner and—more recently— Stefan George. I remember no instance in which this youth movement protested against the rise of National Socialism, while there is evidence that it amply contributed to the ranks of Hitler's supporters. The same romantic nihilism spoke as follows on the rise of Hitler to power in 1934 through Oswald Spengler: 'Man is a beast of prey . . . would be moralists . . . are only beasts of prey with their teeth broken . . . remember the larger beasts of prey are *noble* creatures . . . without the hypocrisy of human morals due to weakness.' [1]

Nazi fanaticism was rooted in the same conviction of the irrelevance of moral motives in public life, which Marxism had expressed in terms of historic materialism, and which caused Marx to eliminate furiously any appeals to moral ideals from his manifestos. Fascists believed with Marx that such moral appeals were but rationalizations of power. Hence their con-tempt of moralizing and their moral justifications of violence as the only honest mode of political action.

Such is the kinship between the ideas which gained fanatical support among revolutionaries and broad influence on the masses of our age. Such the convincing power of an inversion by which scepticism and moral passions reinforce each other in acting on minds whose moral convictions are hamstrung by scepticism. Revolutionary régimes admittedly continue to rule by oppressive violence; but their immense efforts of propaganda

---

[1] Oswald Spengler, *The Hour of Decision* (1934) quoted by Leslie Paul, *The Annihilation of Man* (London, 1944), p. 128.

show that they rely on violence only in combination with the power of their ideas.

Whether we are to fight or to submit—to live or to die—our first duty must be to recognize the awful fact that these ideas are highly stable and seductive. And we must face also the fact that their force and seduction is not due—at least not primarily due—to an evocation of evil instincts, but is gained by satisfying in its own manner the same ideals which we ourselves hold and which we are defending against their attack.

So much in answer of the first part of our question. It explains how the world came to be where it is—divided as it is.

Now the second part of the question: Where does the world go from here? I must not respond to this without first making clear some obvious limitations of any answer I may give to it. The process of inversion which I have described has not taken place everywhere—this is precisely why the world is divided today. Even many revolutionary régimes of the twentieth century are untouched by inversion. Most of the new Asiatic and African countries have achieved independence upholding the traditional ideals of liberalism; I cannot take into account here the wide variety of conditions in these countries. Nor can I deal in detail with the great differences between the Communist countries, ranging from fanatical fury in China to the mere ritual observance of Marxism in Yugoslavia. I can only suggest that these differences be analysed in terms of the trends which I am trying to identify. Finally, though I may tell which way the world is going, I cannot prophesy where it will arrive.

I believe that the predominant trend of human thought in the last ten years has been a retreat from the most extreme forms of inversion. The belief that the rule of the Communist Party embodies all the hopes of humanity, and that its very existence is a full compensation for the fact that it does not fulfil them; that its successes should be ascribed to its peculiar excellence, while its failure be always regarded as incidental—this bias which thrives on its own absurdity, by rendering itself totally unapproachable to argument; this peculiar milieu of the twentieth century which protects its own blazing credulity by a steel armour of scepticism; this condition which is capable of combining highest intelligence and morality in a teaching which reduces them both to epiphenomena of power and profit it is no longer as stable and seductive as it used to be.

This has been no mere weakening due to lassitude. It was a reaffirmation of truth and of morality and the arts, as intrinsic powers of the mind that caused the leading Hungarian Communist intellectuals to rebel against a régime which had showered them with benefits. This reaffirmation was momentous, not only because those who uttered it were abandoning a place in the sun for the shadow of death, but because it was the outcome of a bitter internal struggle in minds divided between two irreconcilable conceptions of conscience. This liberation and re-establishment of thought from its reduction to the functions of ideology has been the mainspring of all revisionism within the Soviet empire, and of the many defections from 'the god that failed' throughout the world.

This movement took on many forms, because any conviction that acknowledges the power of thought in its own right could equally express it. The beliefs to which the modern mind turns beyond nihilism, comprise all the main ideas which prevailed before the descent into nihilism. In my paper I gave a list of three, each defined by its historic past: nationalism, religion and sceptical enlightenment. Today I would add two more, namely romantic enlightenment and its descendant, modern existentialism. But the list is inexhaustible. A man who has broken out of prison might be found in any place to which he had access before he was imprisoned.

Some of those criticizing nationalism or religion seem to have thought that they were opposing my apologia of them. But I had merely said that minds recoiling from nihilism sometimes have done so by renewing their national or religious dedication, and I have spoken in the same breath also of sceptical enlightenment. I said that:

'... the sceptical mood of the enlightenment itself has been given a new lease of life. The more sober pragmatist attitude towards public affairs which has spread since 1950 through England and America, Germany and Austria reproduces in its repudiation of ideological strife the attitude of Voltaire and the Encyclopedists towards religious bigotry.'

This was indeed the only path in which I saw a hope for the future. 'Perhaps,' I said, 'the present recoil may be stabilized by the upsurge of a more clear-sighted political conscience.' And I quoted as an example the way religious conflict had eventually been overcome in England and America.

'Civility prevailed over religious strife and a society was founded which was dynamic and yet united. May not Europe repeat this feat? May we not learn from the disasters of the past forty years to establish a civic partnership, united in its resolve on continuous reforms—our dynamism restrained by the knowledge that radicalism will throw us back into disaster the moment we try to act out its principles literally?'

I have repeated these words here in reply to Sidney Hook's essay 'Enlightenment and Radicalism' in which he too recommends a return to Enlightenment as a cure to our age, and—curiously—conveys this by a strong attack on my supposed denigration of the ideals of Enlightenment. This is due to the fact that he identifies these ideals with the American and British systems of continuous reform through self-government, while on the other hand he thinks that 'the chief causes of the Bolshevik and Nazi revolutions have very little to do with doctrinal beliefs. They are to be found in the First World War and its consequences'. So when I say that the catastrophes of the twentieth century were a manifestation 'of a sceptical rationalism combined with a secularized fervour of Christianity' he believes that I am attacking rationalism—just as other authors have thought that I am attacking Christianity; while I have done neither.

In any case, whatever the proximate causes of our recent revolutions may have been, I think Sidney Hook would agree that their ideas, and the ideas represented by the Soviet government in particular, are still powerful and menacing. My analysis recognizes that they possess this force and seductiveness only because they are deeply rooted in ideas which we share—and because we have also the same ancestry, which first laid the twin burdens of scepticism and social morality on mankind. If this is true, the impasse of completely different languages of which President Kennedy spoke, may not be unbridgeable. If the ideas so hostile to us derive their power from their kinship to our own, we might recognize in them also our own problems. We shall then make contact with the internal difficulties of the Soviet mind which are leading it to revisionism. And we shall no longer see this process then merely as a weakening of our opponents, but recognize it as a struggle of minds like our own against a predicament similar to our own. The revisionist who breaks up the Marxist inversion of moral passions and recoils

o   195

from its political immoralism, returns to our situation in which objectivism conflicts with the claims of moral judgment. He comes up then against our own problems.

A revisionist may expose the logical contradiction in Marxism in terms very similar to those of the academic critics I have quoted. Kolakowski says to the orthodox Communist:

> 'You do not let me measure your moves with a measuring rod of absolute values because in your opinion such values do not exist at all or are purely imagined. But on the other hand, you yourself talk about all human values which must be absolute; thus silently you introduce into your doctrine axiomatic absolutism in a vague and equivocal way in order to destroy it immediately with "historical relativism".'[1]

And in him—a Communist who has survived Stalinism—this insight is far more vivid than it is in us. Problems which to us are speculative, are re-opened by him as wounds, seemingly healed, that have started festering. This can teach those who take the foundations of liberalism to be self-evident, that they are in fact driven by a contradiction which only a faith more experienced than ours can validly transcend.

The problem of modern man is then everywhere the same. He must restore the balance between his critical powers and his moral demands—both of which are more relentless than ever. This may be the starting-point for a movement of intellectual solidarity between the civilizations arising beyond nihilism and the lands which have been spared the political consummation of nihilism. The common ground of this movement would overcome the division of the two mutually exclusive languages and might eventually guide our statesmen to find a way to coexistence and joint progress.

[1] L. Kolakowski, 'Responsibility and History', *Nowa Kultura*, September 1, 1957, Warsaw, Quoted by *East Europe*, December 1957, p. 12.

Biographical Notes

KATHLEEN BLISS: General Secretary of the Church of England Board of Education, Research Officer of Talks Department, B.B.C., editor of *The Christian News-Letter*. Author of *The Service and Status of Women in the Churches*.

ENZO BOERI: Director of the Institute of Human Physiology at the University of Ferrara, Italy; Biologist at the National Research Council of Naples University. Has published various scientific articles in Italy, France, England and the United States.

FRANÇOIS BONDY: Swiss essayist and journalist, Director of Publications of the Congress for Cultural Freedom.

A. K. BROHI: Pakistani jurist, High Commissioner for Pakistan in India. Has published *An Adventure in Self-Expression* and *Fundamental Law of Pakistan*.

FRANCOIS FEJTO: Journalist and writer, commentator on foreign policy at Agence France Presse. Author of *Printemps des Peuples, Histoire des Démocraties Populaires, Dieu et son Juif*, etc.

PIETER GEYL: Professor of History at the Universities of London and Utrecht up to 1958, author of many historical works, among which *Use and Abuse of History, Revolt of the Netherlands*, etc.

HELMUT GOLLWITZER: Professor of Theology at the Free University of Berlin; author of *Die christliche Gemeinde in der Politischen Welt, Die Christen und die Atomwaffen*.

INGEMAR HEDENIUS: Professor of Philosophy at Uppsala University, author of *Sensationalism and Theology in Berkeley's Philosophy, Studies in Hume's Ethics, On Law and Morals, In Search for a View of Life* and other works.

RICHARD HENSMAN: Singhalese writer and journalist, Research Secretary for the Overseas Council, London, and editor of *Community*.

JEANNE HERSCH: Professor of Philosophy, University of Geneva. Author of *L'Illusion philosophique, Idéologies et Réalité*, etc.

WALTHER HOFER: Professor of Political Science at the University of Berne. Has published important collections of documents on the history of the Third Reich: *Deutsche Geschichte, 1933-1939* and *Dokumente des Nationalsozialismus*, which have been translated into English, Italian and Japanese.

Biographical Notes

SIDNEY HOOK: Professor of Philosophy at New York University. Author of *From Hegel to Marx, Education for Modern Man, Heresy Yes—Conspiracy No, Political Power and Personal Freedom*, etc.

ALBERT HOURANI: Professor of Modern History of the Near East; Fellow of St. Antony's College, Oxford. Has published various books on the problems of the Arab world, such as *Syria and Lebanon* and *Minorities in the Arab World*.

PAUL IGNOTUS: author and journalist, senior editor of *Irodalmi Ujsag* (The Hungarian Literary Gazette, London). Has published a number of books, among which *La Responsabilità degli Intellettuali* and *Political Prisoner*.

FRODE JAKOBSEN: Member of the Danish Parliament; author, among other works, of *Europe and Denmark, The European Movement and the Council of Europe*.

K. A. JELENSKI: Polish essayist and literary critic now living in Paris, author of *La Realta Dell'ottobre Polacco*, has contributed articles to *Encounter, Partisan Review, Preuves, Der Monat*, etc.

HANS KOHN: Professor of History at City College, New York. Author of numerous books, among which *The Mind of Germany, Is the Liberal West in Decline?*

THEODOR LITT: Professor of Philosophy. Between *Erkenntnis und Leben*, published in 1923, and *Fuhren oder Wachsealassen*, published in 1960, has written a considerable number of essays and philosophical works of which the best known is *Hegel*. He taught for several years in Eastern Germany.

KARL LOEWITH: Professor at Heidelberg University. Has published numerous works, among which *From Hegel to Nietzsche, Meaning in History* and *Wissen, Glaube und Skepsis*.

RICHARD LOWENTHAL: Professor of Political Science, Fall University, Berlin. Journalist and writer, frequent contributor to *The Observer*.

HERBERT LÜTHY: Professor of History at the Swiss Federal Polytechnical School. After *Montaigne* (essays), published in 1953, and *A l'Heure de son Clocher* (essay on France), has published an important book on *The Protestant Bank in France from the Revocation of the Edict of Nantes to the Revolution*.

SALVADOR DE MADARIAGA: Spanish statesman and former Ambassador, now living in exile. He is the author of numerous books on history and political science, among which the most important are: *Spaniards, Englishmen and Frenchmen, Spain*, an essay on contemporary history, *Christopher Columbus* and *Portrait of Europe*.

CZESLAW MILOSZ: Polish poet, essayist and novelist, author of *The Captive Mind, La Prise du Pouvoir, Sur les Bords de l'Issa*, etc., now professor of Slavic literatures, University of California, Berkeley.

EHSAN NARAGHI: Professor of Sociology at Teheran University. Has published several works on the Middle East.

JAYAPRAKASH NARAYAN: Indian statesman, retired from active politics in 1952 to join the Bhoodan (Land Gift) movement.

ROBERT OPPENHEIMER: Physicist, Director of the Institute for Advanced Study, Princeton, U.S.A.

JOSEF PIEPER: Professor of Philosophy at Münster University. Has written various books, amongst which *Grundformen sozialer Spielregeln, Was heisst Philosophieren?* and *Ueber den Begriff der Tradition.*

MICHAEL POLANYI: turned to Philosophy after having been Professor of Physics and Professor of Economics. Fellow of Merton College, Oxford. Author of *U.S.S.R. Economics, Money and Unemployment* (diagrammatic film), *The Contempt of Freedom, Full Employment and Free Trade, Science, Faith and Society, Logic of Liberty, Personal Knowledge, The Study of Man,* etc.

RAJA RAO: Indian writer, came to Europe at the age of 19, studying literature at the University of Montpellier and at the Sorbonne. He published his first stories in French and English. His best known book is *The Serpent and the Rope.*

RONALD SEGAL: the South African radical writer and journalist, is now editor and publisher of *Africa South in Exile,* published in London.

HUGH SETON-WATSON: Professor at the London School of Slavonic Studies. Author of several books on history and Eastern Europe, he has recently published in London a book on the international situation, *Neither Peace nor War.*

ALTIERO SPINELLI: Italian publicist, delegate of the *Congrès du Peuple Européen,* author of *Manifesto dei Federalisti Europei, L'Europa non cade dal Cielo,* etc.

MICHIO TAKEYAMA: writer, lecturer at the University of Tokyo, editor of the magazine *Jiyu.*

ALEX WEISSBERG-CYBULSKI: physicist and writer, directed the Kharkov Institute of Physical Research until his imprisonment during the Soviet purges. His experience is described in his book *The Witches' Sabbath.*

Index

201

Index